The Young Adult's Guide to Being a Great Waiter or Waitress

Everything
You Need to Know
to Earn Better Tips

By Atlantic Publishing
Editorial Staff

The Young Adult's Guide to Being a Great Waiter or Waitress: Everything You Need to Know to Earn Better Tips

Copyright © 2017 Atlantic Publishing Group, Inc.
1405 SW 6th Avenue • Ocala, Florida 34471 • Phone 800-814-1132 • Fax 352-622-1875
Website: www.atlantic-pub.com • Email: sales@atlantic-pub.com
SAN Number: 268-1250

Library of Congress Cataloging-in-Publication Data

The young adult's guide to being a great waiter and waitress : everything you need to know to earn better tips.
    pages cm
  Includes bibliographical references and index.
  ISBN 978-1-60138-991-6 (alk. paper) -- ISBN 1-60138-991-4 (alk. paper) 1. Table service--Vocational guidance. 2. Waiters. 3. Waitresses. I. Atlantic Publishing Group. II. Title: Guide to being a great waiter and waitress.
  TX925.Y68 2015
  642'.6023--dc23
                          2015034817

Printed in the United States

PROJECT MANAGER AND EDITOR: Rebekah Sack • rsack@atlantic-pub.com
COVER DESIGN: Jackie Miller • millerjackiej@gmail.com
INTERIOR LAYOUT AND JACKET DESIGN: Antoinette D'Amore • addesign@videotron.ca

Printed on Recycled Paper

Reduce. Reuse. RECYCLE.

A decade ago, Atlantic Publishing signed the Green Press Initiative. These guidelines promote environmentally friendly practices, such as using recycled stock and vegetable-based inks, avoiding waste, choosing energy-efficient resources, and promoting a no-pulping policy. We now use 100-percent recycled stock on all our books. The results: in one year, switching to post-consumer recycled stock saved 24 mature trees, 5,000 gallons of water, the equivalent of the total energy used for one home in a year, and the equivalent of the greenhouse gases from one car driven for a year.

Over the years, we have adopted a number of dogs from rescues and shelters. First there was Bear and after he passed, Ginger and Scout. Now, we have Kira, another rescue. They have brought immense joy and love not just into our lives, but into the lives of all who met them.

We want you to know a portion of the profits of this book will be donated in Bear, Ginger and Scout's memory to local animal shelters, parks, conservation organizations, and other individuals and nonprofit organizations in need of assistance.

*– **Douglas & Sherri Brown,***
President & Vice-President of Atlantic Publishing

Table of Contents

Introduction

Perhaps you've heard the server nightmares. You got three tables at once, the old guy in the corner needs another side of ranch, the busboy is nowhere to be found, the bartender lost your drink ticket, you just got another table, the kitchen is running 45 minutes per order, and there's a 6-month old screaming at table 2.

A quick online search of "server nightmares" pulls up article after article of dreams that are now being referred to as "waitmares." Jeremy Holm, a 30-year veteran of the service industry (oh, and an actor in *House of Cards*, no big deal) recalls a particularly vivid one, "The restaurant's set up, but there are no other servers there, and suddenly there a lot of guests coming in. And it's just assumed that I'm waiting on the whole restaurant."[1]

It's no doubt that being a waiter or waitress can be stressful. However, there are definite pros, too — having cash on hand after every shift you work isn't so bad, right?

This book is going to cover everything you need to know about being a great waiter or waitress. You'll discover tips and tricks to impress not only your boss, but your customers, too. A lot of research has been done on how to increase your tips, which is really a direct reflection of how well you're doing your job (except for that one guy that always leaves a quarter). We'll uncover all of that, so put your apron on and get ready to blow everyone away.

Hashtag server life.

I mean #serverlife.

1.   Furino, 2015.

Chapter 1

Why Should I Be a Server?

There are a lot of reasons to start your working life out in a restaurant. In fact, a lot of service-industry veterans say that it's almost a right of passage. There a lot of life lessons to be learned in a restaurant (insert eye roll here). But seriously, waiting on tables will develop your patience and your ability to adapt, your people-person skills will start impressing your mom, your work ethic will improve, you'll get better at multi-tasking, and honestly, the list really does go on.

Being a server builds character, and at the end of the day, if you can weasel your way into the right joint, you can make pretty good money doing it. Take a look at this pros and cons list of why you should (or shouldn't) consider waiting tables.[2]

PROS	CONS
You always have cash with you	You might always spend your cash on hand
You get paid every day you work	No benefits
You're always around people	You pretty much have to work weekends
A better job equals a better income	Dealing with really rude people and possibly becoming bitter
You're constantly on your feet	You might start developing back or knee issues

As with any service industry job that requires you to be constantly happy, attentive, and active, there are going to be some drawbacks. It can be really difficult to be all smiles when you're not exactly so happy. Like when you have a huge final exam the next day and Jackie wouldn't cover your shift for you. But if you think the service industry is a good fit for you (at least for now), you should take a moment to evaluate yourself. Are you marketable? Will the hiring manager want to hire you?

Let's take a look at a list of qualities restaurants look for when hiring their waitstaff.

What Makes A Good Server?

Servers are the link between the restaurant's customers and sales, so your future employers will be looking for a server who is going to be successful at marketing the menu to the guests. Obviously, knowledge and experience make a great server, but what character traits are they looking for?

Effective communicator

One of a server's main jobs is to communicate with customers and the rest of the staff. Servers should be able to communicate with a wide range of personalities. This includes facial expressions and body language. If a server is frowning at a guest, he or she is communicating negative emotions. A natural smile implies a welcoming emotion.

Fast Fact

Introducing yourself by name has been scientifically proven to increase your tips by about 8 percent. When you greet your table, say something like, "Good evening. My name is Kelly, and I'll be serving you tonight. Have you been here before?"[3]

High energy

Restaurant serving is a tough job that requires many hours of walking and long periods on your feet. Servers need to be able to maintain this energy level throughout a shift. You should also be prepared for little to no breaks during a shift. Investing in some comfortable nonslip shoes is a really good idea — foot inserts can also make your shift that much more cozy.

Flexibility

Servers should be flexible and should be able to deal with sudden, unexpected rushes. They also need to be flexible and understanding when dealing with customers. Get ready for your boss to call you on Friday night asking if you can fill in for Brad who called in sick. Also get ready customers that do things like order a salad and then complain that there are onions on it (even when they never said no onions). Being flexible is an absolute requirement.

Can handle stress

The restaurant world is a stressful one, and servers will have to deal with physical and mental stress on a daily basis. This stress can take the form of annoying customers, a sassy kitchen crew, another server that won't pull his or her own weight, or simply dealing with a full restaurant.

You should also keep in mind that many restaurant managers work upwards of 50-60 hours per week. Be mindful of their potential stress levels.

Cooperative

Restaurants require a good deal of teamwork and cooperation. Therefore, servers should be willing to pitch in and help. For example, a good server will help the salad person when she is backed up; a less than ideal server would stand and wait for the salads. You, my friend, are not less than ideal.

Courteous

Servers should be polite and courteous with their managers, fellow employees, and guests. Nothing is worse than a bitter server complaining under her breath every five seconds about how much she hates her job. Don't be that girl. Or guy.

Desire to please others

A server must be able to put his or her ego in check for the good of the customer as well as for the good of the tip. If you particularly respond to positive feedback, serving might be your calling. One of the most exciting parts of waiting tables is that you're literally working for your paycheck — if you have that inner desire to make people happy, you're a natural, and the money will follow.

Empathic

Good servers can read a customer quickly and can see if they want to be alone or are interested in chatting. This ability to sense another person's mood is helpful for setting the right tone for a guest. If a solitary diner is reading, the server shouldn't hang around just because he or she assumes the guest is lonely. If the guest encourages conversation, that's fine; otherwise, he or she may simply be interested in the book they've brought along.

Neat and clean appearance

Servers need to be neat and clean. Your appearance indicates to the guests how clean and organized the restaurant is. If a server runs up to the table frantically searching for a pen wearing a dirty apron and shirt, the customer is going to feel that the restaurant itself is dirty. You are a reflection of the establishment, so not only is your tip at stake, but the reputation of the company is as well.

Fast Fact

A French study showed that 50 percent more men left a tip if the waitress was wearing makeup, and the average tip was 26 percent more. Another study found that red lipstick increased tips as well.[4]

Giving Awesome Service

Now you have a pretty good idea of the qualities a hiring manager will be looking for, and that's great. But to make sure you get hired, you should be familiar with how to give great service. The hiring manager might say something like, "What's the most important part of being a great server?" or "Explain great service to me."

Well, don't worry. Here are 14 things you should know about giving memorable service.

Smile

This is one of the simplest yet most important things you can do. Smiling sets the tone and makes everyone more comfortable. If you look less than pleased and have an attitude, customers may leave you a bad tip, or worse, never come back to the restaurant.

A ton of studies have shown that smiling has a direct correlation to better tips. Think about the last time you went to a restaurant and had a great experience — the server was probably really pleasant, and chances are that he or she was smiling quite a bit. This one is just too easy to pass up — and if you're in a horrible mood, fake it to make it, baby.

Keep yourself updated

Make sure you're always on top of today's specials, new menu items, dishes that are 86'd, and so on. Nothing is worse than telling a customer about an awesome dish and then realizing a few minutes later that you don't serve it anymore or that you're out of the main ingredient. Walking up to a table with confident knowledge of what's going on will make your life so much easier.

There is no agreed-upon etymology for the word "86'd," which is a term restaurants and bars use to express that something is out of stock or that someone should be cut off. Popular theories[5] of the term's origin include the following:

1. During Prohibition (when alcohol was illegal), there was a bar called Chumley's, which was located at 86 Bedford Street in New York City. In order to stay in business, the bar would work with the police so that they might be warned of possible raids. At Chumley's, the police would call and tell the bartender to "86 his customers." This meant that a

raid would happen soon and that the customers should leave via the 86 Bedford door.

2. The United States Navy had a coding system called "Allowance Type" which was abbreviate to "AT." This system was used to keep track of inventory. The code "AT-6" was assigned to inventory that was supposed to be thrown away or disposed of. It's pretty easy to see how "AT-6" could be slowly known as "86."

3. Another possible explanation is that up until the 1980s, whiskey used to come in 100 or 86 proof. When a bartender thought a customer had a bit too much to drink of the heavier stuff (the 100 proof), they would start serving them the less-potent stuff (the 86 proof). In bar lingo, one would say that the person had been "86'd."

4. Most graves are eight feet long and six feet deep. If something has been "put to death," one might conclude it has been "86'd."

Recognition

Recognition is very important, and this can be as simple as addressing the customer by name. You can do this a number of ways — you can introduce yourself and ask for their name as well, or you can wait until they pay (hopefully with a credit card) to say something like, "Thank you so much Mr. Trump. Have a great day."

Not that you'd be waiting on the president, but you get the idea.

Listen to your customers

It's way better to overcommunicate than to drop the ball. You may want to repeat information back to customers, especially if the order is detailed. This will let the guest know you wrote it down correctly.

Patrons will appreciate your attention to detail. Nothing is worse than thinking that head nod meant, "Yes, I want another beer," and then delivering it to a seemingly annoyed customer that says something like, "I didn't order that."

Alrighty then.

Make eye contact

In American culture, people tend to trust others that look you in the eye. Look directly at the customer you are addressing. Give your guests your undivided attention, and let them know that you're listening. Don't stare at the table, the floor, or the artwork on the wall. Clear your head, smile, and pay attention. Make sure you're at the table when you're talking. Don't talk to your guests as you're flying by; it makes people feel unimportant, and no one likes that feeling.

Learn shorthand codes

All restaurants use shorthand on their guest checks to communicate information. It's quicker than writing everything out. Ask what the common shorthand codes are. If your restaurant uses paper checks to fill orders, this is extremely important. If your restaurant has a system set in place that only requires you to type in an order on a screen, you need to make sure that you understand your shorthand so you don't ring in the wrong thing.

Ask other servers what they do — they may have some time saving techniques such as "FF" for "French fries" or "MW B w/ LTOP" for "Medium Well Burger with Lettuce, Tomato, Onion, and Pickle."

Rules of the road

Learn the set traffic rules in your establishment to make sure that aisles don't become clogged. For example, if two servers are heading for the same table, the first one should go to farthest side of the table. Always let the guest go first.

Rules of recovery

Accidents are bound to happen, but how you handle the accident is the most important thing. First, promptly offer an honest, sincere apology. Second, take steps to resolve the problem.

Let's say you spill tomato bisque on the white shirt of one of your lunch customers. You should immediately help clean up the customer; then, you or a manager should offer to pay for the dry cleaning. Suggest that the customer send you the bill, and you can take care of it for them. If a customer's food is wrong or prepared incorrectly, immediately get the food to the guest who has had to wait. Any situation can be made right, but it's always good practice to go to a manager first and explain what has happened.

Be courteous

It may seem like common sense, but it's amazing how many servers don't treat guests with common courtesy. Make sure you say "Thank you" and "You're welcome." The terms "ma'am" and "sir" are often appropriate as well, especially with older guests.

Be knowledgeable

One of the best resources you have for increasing your tips is to be knowledgeable about the menu. You should be able to tell a guest if the soup of the day is cream-based or if the shrimp is sautéed or grilled. Use adjectives when describing menu items; you want to provide the customer with a mouth-watering mental image.

For example, try saying, "Our special tonight is a rack of lamb, braised in a Merlot and rosemary broth and served with a savory wild mushroom bread pudding and fresh-roasted asparagus." You should also be well informed about the establishment itself and should be able to answer questions such as operating hours, which credit cards are accepted, and types of service available.

Acknowledge the customer quickly

Customers need to be acknowledged within 30-60 seconds of being seated. Don't leave them waiting. Waiting will negatively affect a customer's mood, and a guest's mood is highly likely to affect your tip. If you can't get there as quickly as you'd like, you should acknowledge the customer's existence by stopping by and saying something like, "I'll be right with you."

Up-selling

Up-selling will increase tips, because you're increasing the total amount of the sale, and most people tip on a percentage of the total. Suggest appetizers, desserts, and premium drinks, but don't annoy the guest.

For instance, if a customer orders a gin and tonic, you could say, "Tanqueray?" This simple suggestion may influence a customer to order the more expensive brand rather than the well brand.

Fast Fact

A "well" drink is the cheapest liquor available at the bar. The term comes from "the well," which is the place where the bartender has mixers and the most frequently poured liquors. They're in the space that is most easily accessed for the quickest service.

Be on good terms with the back of the house

If a customer gets the wrong order or if their food is not prepared as they requested, you have to tell the kitchen to remake the food, right? If you're on good terms with the kitchen staff, they'll be happy to help you. It's always a good idea to be on good terms with the cooks and the busboys. Odds are you're going to need their help, and they'll be more likely to do a favor if you're a nice, decent person.

Show gratitude

People are dealing with a lot in their lives, and you have a chance to make their day. Express gratitude in the tone of your voice when you thank them for eating at your restaurant. Making them feel appreciated will help them to remember you. Suggest that they ask for you when they come back again.

Types of Restaurants

Before you apply to a restaurant, you should have a general idea of the options you have. There are three main types of restaurants: fine dining, bistro/trattorias, and family.

Fine dining

These restaurants usually offer fine china and table linens in a luxurious surrounding. A host (or mâitre d') is in charge of captains, servers, bus people, and sommeliers (wine stewards). The menu is usually extensive, as is the wine list. The pace of service in a fine-dining establishment is leisurely with meals often lasting up to three hours. Also, it's stinkin' expensive.

Fine dining restaurants only account for about 10 percent of total U.S. restaurant sales.[6]

Bistro/Trattoria

This type covers a range of restaurants from white tablecloth establishments with a range of menu styles to more simple venues. Traditionally, bistros/trattorias were family-operated, but now, the term generally refers to any simple restaurant.

Family

These restaurants include family-style, diners, and themed restaurants. These restaurants usually do not have linens or fine china, the food is fairly simple, and the staff often has less experience than at the above-mentioned types of restaurants. Think of typical chain-restaurants. This is most likely the type of restaurant you will be starting at.

Staff Positions and Duties

All restaurants have the same basic front-of-the-house positions, but finer dining establishments will have a more extensive staff. In all three of the main restaurant types you are likely to find a general manager, dining room managers, hosts, servers, bartenders (if the restaurant serves alcohol) and bus people (also called server assistants). In fine-dining establishments, however, you may also find a wine steward and a captain. Let's take a bit of a closer look at the different positions in a restaurant. After all, you may be climbing the ladder shortly!

General Manager

The GM is responsible for the entire operation. This person is responsible for the overall management of the dining room and bar services, including facility management and public relations.

Dining Room Manager

This person is in charge of dining room service. Some of his or her duties include maintaining operating cost records, hiring and training front-of-the-house employees, working with serving staff to ensure quality food and beverage presentation, ensuring proper food-handling procedures, handling guest complaints, and helping to plan menus.

Captain

The person in this position is usually responsible for service in a particular section of tables. He or she may take orders and assist the servers in that section. Since the captain is ultimately responsible for the service in that section, he or she rarely leaves the floor.

Host

The host greets and seats customers, takes phone reservations, and looks after the front lobby area. (In casual restaurants, this position usually takes the place of the general manager or captain.) The host or hostess will also assign service stations to all servers and bussers, inform servers of menu changes and daily specials, provide menus to guests, and manage special seating requests of guests.

Wine Steward

This person is responsible for the creation of a wine list, maintaining the wine inventory, recommending wines to customers, and serving bottled wine.

Head Waiter

This person may also be known as a maître d'. He or she manages a restaurant's dining room to ensure that guests have a pleasant dining experience. The tasks undertaken by the head waiter include ensuring that waiters and waitresses are quick on their feet and able to answer customer enquiries on the day's dishes, ensuring dishes arrive promptly, ensuring that staff are dressed properly, organizing the wait system, and supervising the restaurant clean-up and closing duties.

Server

A server is responsible for coordinating serving stations and providing customers with quality service. His or her primary duties include: greet guests and provide them with menu information, including preparation techniques, specials and wine pairings; communicate with dining room and kitchen personnel; take food and drink orders; serve food and beverages; total bill and accept payment; stock their station; and perform assigned side duties.

Bus Person/Server Assistant

Bus people and server assistants help servers to maintain service efficiency and ensure guest satisfaction by maintaining cleanliness of the front-of-the-house area. He or she greets guests appropriately when they are seated; communicates with the host or hostess and waitstaff to maintain service efficiency and ensures guest satisfaction; maintains cleanliness and sanitation of the front-of-the-house including all tables, chairs, floors, windows, and restrooms; removes dirty dishes and utensils from tables between courses; clears tables after guests leave; and may help waitstaff in serving tables with hot beverages such as coffee or tea.

Hopefully you've chosen the restaurant you want to apply to and have nailed that interview. Are you ready to start training? The next chapter will guide you through your first day. Get ready to make a great first impression!

---

2.   A lot of the concepts in the chart come from The Waitress Confessions, 2015.
3.   Lynn, 1996.
4.   Shin, 2014.
5.   McGough, 2013.
6.   WebstaurantStore, 2016.

Chapter 2

Your First Day

So, you've been hired and you're officially a server in training. There are a lot of common knowledge tips we'll go over in this chapter, but there are also some tips that you might not be aware of. Being in the service industry can be a really great time, so follow these easy suggestions to make sure you're making the best impression.

Know Your Schedule

Don't be that guy that shows up at the wrong time or forgets the days they're supposed to work. If your restaurant posts the schedule on a bulletin board, take a picture of it. If they utilize a scheduling app such as HotSchedules, make sure to check it every day to ensure nothing has changed.

On the other end of the spectrum, you don't want to get ready and drive to work only to realize you work tomorrow, not today. Make your life easy by making sure you know your schedule for the week. One final tip: If you need to check your schedule, don't call during a busy time of the day. A general rule of thumb is to call between 2–4 p.m. or after 9 p.m.

Don't Show Up Late

Perhaps you've heard the famous saying: Show up 10 minutes early, you're on time. Show up on time, you're late. Show up late, don't bother showing up at all.

You might be able to start showing up closer to the actual time you're scheduled later on, but at first, you should definitely be arriving at least 10 minutes early to your shift. Some managers will want you to clock in no earlier than five minutes early for your shift (to make sure you're not eating up the time clock for a few extra bucks), but it's always a good idea to plan on showing up earlier than you think is necessary. This will impress any boss in any line of work (for the record).

In the United States, there are approximately 14 million employees in the restaurant industry. That number is predicted to rise to over 16 million by 2026.[7]

Pick Up the Pace

You should be at a fast walk at all times. Don't be that server that's in everyone's way. Get used to hustling. Don't let your guests wait on you. You'll also make better relationships with your coworkers if you're constantly picking up your pace.

For example, Christopher's table flags you down and asks for ketchup. You could do one of two things — you could go grab that Diet Coke you've been craving for the past five minutes and then saunter back to the kitchen for the bottle, or you could hustle there and back. Christopher will like you a lot more if you hustle.

Don't Be a Gossiper

Restaurant managers hate it when servers huddle in a corner and gossip. You should constantly be looking for something to do, something to clean, tables to help, trash to clean up, and so on. There is pretty much always something to be done in a restaurant, so wasting your time spreading rumors about who got fired last week is never a good idea.

Get Ready For Side Work

Be prepared to do side work, which is also sometimes called "cut work," or little jobs you do during your shift and when you get cut. This usually consists of taking out trash, sweeping or vacuuming under your tables, filling the ice, wiping down the walls, rolling silverware, and so on. You might have already known this, but being aware that serving tables is much more than just dropping off checks and filling up drinks is important.

You may be asked to do things you really don't want to do, like unclogging that drain or plunging that toilet, but whatever you do, don't complain about it. It's just part of the job.

Don't Ask Lame Questions

You're new. Don't get on your manager's bad side just yet. Don't ask the following questions:

1. When will I be cut?
2. Can I eat that?
3. What's my discount?
4. Can I have this day, this day, and this day off?

In general, managers don't like it when you ask what time you'll be cut. To them, this is like nagging. They'll tell you when you're done. Leave it alone, and be patient.

No, you can't eat that. You're working. Stop it. Put the fry down.

Asking about the server discount is a valid question, but it can come across the wrong way. Wait until someone tells you, or wait until the end of your shift when you're thinking about ordering food. You'll avoid making someone annoyed unnecessarily.

Writing "thank you" on the back of the check can raise your tip by an easy 2 percent.[8]

Don't start requesting off a bunch of days right away. The longer you work there, the more willing the management will be to give you off special days such as holiday weekends or busy times of the year, like graduation. However, doing this right away sets the tone for how potentially annoying and troublesome you will be. It can be difficult for a manager to make a schedule that everyone is happy with anyway, but when Jessica requested off the entire weekend and Chad can only work lunch shifts, it becomes even more difficult.

Now that you have an idea of what you should do on your first day, let's get in to some specifics — hosting and making sure guests feel welcome.

---

7. Mealey, 2016.
8. Shin, 2014.

Chapter 3

Hosting and Welcoming Guests

Every employee in a restaurant is a host, and the customer is your guest. Generally, the host or hostess greets the customers as they enter the dining room and takes them to their tables. However, when the host is busy or there isn't a host (which can happen on slower days), it becomes the waitstaff's responsibility to meet and seat customers. The guest's first impressions of their dining experience fall right here, so it's important to get it right.

The world's largest restaurant is in Damascus, Syria. It has 6,014 seats.[9]

Fast Fact

The main purpose of the host or hostess, as the name suggests, is to provide hospitality. Acting as the representative of the management of the business, he or she should greet customers and try to make them feel that they are welcomed guests.

The host or hostess has the responsibility of giving customers the impression, as soon as they enter the restaurant, that they may expect good service. The host or hostess shares responsibility with the server for the customers' satisfaction with the service they receive. A pleasant reception, careful service throughout the meal, and courteous treatment as they leave will impress customers and make them feel appreciated.

As you read this chapter, try to read it with two things in mind — you may have to step in to the hosting position from time to time, and you also need to be able to understand what goes into being a great host. You might find yourself getting annoyed when Jen keeps double seating you, but if you fully understand the method to the madness, you'll be able to see the bigger picture.

Duties of the Restaurant Host/Hostess

The host has a lot of duties to perform. In performing these duties, you play an important part in bringing about the kind of service that will satisfy guests.

You represent the management to the customer, you convey the wishes of both the management and the customer to the sales staff and kitchen crew, and you report to the management the compliments, the suggestions, and the complaints of both customers and employees. Good judgment in these relationships is very important.

In your daily work as a host or hostess, you should be familiar with regulations concerning the seating of customers, serving, filling orders in the kitchen, and party service. Make sure you ask the following questions if they're not already answered during your training.

Seating questions

- Is the customer allowed to choose to be served by a particular waitperson?

- During what hours are reservations permitted?
  How long should tables be held?

Serving questions

- What is the method for table setup?
- What specific method of service is used for:
  - A la carte orders?
  - Special parties?
- What is the division of work between the waitstaff and bus
  persons/server assistants? What duties are each expected to
  perform independently? What duties are performed together?
- Are extra servings of hot bread offered? Are second cups of
  coffee allowed without extra charge?
- When and under what conditions may substitutions be
  made on a menu? Is there an extra charge when a guest
  requests a substitution?

Kitchen questions

- What foods does each kitchen station serve?
- What is the best routine for a waitperson to use in
  filling an order?
- To whom at each serving station should the waitperson
  give the order?
- Where are supplies of dishes, glassware, silver, and linen kept?
- Where may extra supplies of butter, cream, ice, crackers, and
  condiments be found?

Large party questions

- What special rooms and dining room spaces may be reserved?
- What is the largest number of persons that can be accommodated? What is the smallest number for which any one room may be reserved?
- At what hours is party service provided? How late may a group remain?
- What is the minimum price for which a special group may be served? What is the usual price?
- What provisions are made for flowers, decorations, or food items that are brought in by guests such as birthday cakes or bottles of champagne?
- Is there a set gratuity for large parties?
- Is a special crew provided for party service?

You are the first member of the restaurant staff whom customers meet as they enter the dining room. For this reason, you should make a good first impression by both your appearance and behavior. Other requirements are that you have good posture, be well groomed, and present a neat and attractive appearance. You should use good English, and always speak in a clear voice.

Half of restaurant-goers say that eating out is an essential part of their lifestyle.[10]

Fast Fact

Editorial Photo Credit: Paul Prescott

In your relationship with the restaurant management as the host or hostess, you should show that you are:

- Loyal to the business and its policies
- Able to follow regulations and carry out directions
- Willing to assume responsibility
- Able to take criticism

In your relationship with customers, you should:

- Be pleasant and show a willingness to be of service
- Be courteous and try to prevent misunderstandings
- Be impartial to prevent charges of favoritism on the part of customers
- Attempt to resolve customer complaints
- Be careful to uphold the high standards of food service

In your contacts with coworkers, you should:

- Be friendly
- Show sincere interest in the restaurant's work
- Be fair in working with associates
- Be good-tempered, even in difficult situations

Inspecting the Dining Room

As the host or hostess, you are responsible for the appearance, cleanliness, and order of the dining room during the serving period. Before the meal service begins, you should check to be sure that:

1. The main dining room, private rooms, booths, and counters are clean and in good order. Any disorder should be reported and fixed before the meal service begins.
2. Window curtains or blinds are adjusted to give good light.
3. The temperature of the dining room is properly adjusted.

4. Tables are arranged properly and are completely equipped.

5. Serving stands and side tables are properly arranged and have adequate supplies.

6. There are enough menu cards, and they are distributed properly.

7. Order forms and sharpened pencils are provided.

8. Table reservations and "reserved" signs have been placed.

9. The tables arranged for special parties are ready, and flowers, candles, and other decorations are set up.

10. Flowers are fresh and nicely arranged.

11. There are enough tablecloths, napkins, and serving towels.

12. There is enough rolled silverware for the evening.

13. Necessary repairs have been made.

Providing Excellent Service

To go above and beyond, you should be mindful of the following:

*   See that orders are taken as soon as customers are ready to give them. When the regular server is unavailable, take the order or direct another server to do so.

*   Notify the server that the customers are ready for service when he or she has been busy elsewhere.

*   Keep customers supplied with water, butter, bread, and hot coffee. Be careful with this, though, as some servers might take offense, with the assumption being that you're doing their job for them. Just check with the server by saying something like, "You wouldn't be offended if I topped off your table's drinks now and again, would you?"

- Give kids special menus, coloring sheets, and gaming tablets as provided by the restaurant.

- Conserve menus and keep them by collecting them from tables and side stands during the meal period.

- Be courteous to all guests, but don't engage in long conversations that take your attention from the service of other guests.

- If time permits, open the door for guests as they leave and say "goodbye."

- Have tables cleared and reset promptly after the guests leave them.

- Check supplies and linen at the close of the meal period to determine the amount on hand. See that they are given proper care and that they are put away correctly.

According to the Guinness Book of World Records, Botin Restaurant is the world's oldest restaurant. It is located in Madrid, Spain, and has been in business since 1725.[11]

Making Arrangements for Special Parties

Unless there is a supervisor in charge of catering, the host generally takes reservations for special parties. You should follow the regulations of the management — concerning maximum and minimum size for special groups, minimum charges, number of courses, food choices allowed at a given price, time, and guarantee of number. You should also obtain the necessary information from the person making the reservation, including:

- Name, address, and telephone number of the person calling
- The name of the organization, if one is involved
- Day, date, and hour of reservation
- Occasion
- Probable number in the group, and number of guests guaranteed
- Preferences as to table location and dining room (Inside or outside? Low or high tables?)
- Price or price range
- Arrangements for flowers and decorations
- Arrangements for payment of the sales check (is the check to be paid in one amount or is the money to be collected individually?)

Serving Special Parties

The general responsibilities of the host for the service of a special party includes duties like:

1. Securing and assigning the extra waitstaff and buspersons needed for service.
2. Rearranging the serving schedule to allow use of regular employees.
3. Giving instructions for setting tables.
4. Checking set tables for completeness, arrangement and appearance.

5. Checking to be sure that the correct number of places has been set.
6. Giving the necessary general instructions to individual servers.
7. Giving specific instructions to individual servers.
8. Notifying the kitchen staff of the time when the service will be required.
9. Approving and supplying special services that may be equested by customers, such as tea instead of coffee, fish instead of meat, bread instead of rolls, and foods for persons on special diets.

Americans spend less on food than ever before. From 1960 to 2007, American food budgets descreased from 17.5 to 9.6 percent.[12]

Fast Fact

Receiving Customers

The host or hostess should receive customers in a gracious, yet dignified manner. You should endeavor to make the guests feel welcome and assured that they will receive satisfactory service. With this in mind, you may:

- Stand near the entrance to the dining room in order to greet customers as they arrive, and seat them promptly.

- Greet the customers with a pleasant smile and nod, using the appropriate greeting — "Good morning," "Good afternoon," or "Good evening" — and greeting customers by name whenever possible.

- Ask how many are in each group, and seat the group at a suitable table. Avoid the use of a table for four to seat one or two persons unless no smaller tables are available.

- Ask the customers' preference with regard to table location when the dining room is not too crowded.

- Walk slightly ahead of the customers when taking them to a table. An easy way to ensure you don't stride way ahead of them is by keeping a conversation going. Turn your head back every few seconds and say something like, "Have you ever been here before?" or "What brings you here today?"

- Seat couples at small tables or in booths. Place disabled and elderly persons near the entrance so they will not be required to walk far. Seat men or women who come alone at small tables, but avoid placing them behind a post, near the entrance doorway, or in the direct path to the kitchen doors.

- Make sure that no one section of the dining room is overcrowded.

- When customers must wait for tables, seat them where they are available, or indicate a place to stand that is out of the way of traffic.

- Have the table cleared of dirty dishes and reset before customers are seated.

- Provide a booster seat for small children and a highchair for infants.

- Place the opened menu before each guest, from the left side, or instruct the waiter to do so.

- Fill the water glasses or instruct the busperson or waitperson to do so promptly.

Hosting is an important part of serving in a restaurant. Whether you start out as a host and work your way up to serving or whether it's a smaller restaurant where servers double as the host, you need to know how to effectively greet customers into your establishment.

Now that we have that out of the way, let's move on to the tips of the trade — how to truly be a great waiter or waitress.

---

9. Mealey, 2016.
10. Reserve, 2016.
11. Mealey, 2016.
12. US Department of Agriculture, 2016.

Chapter 4

Giving Great Service

Being a great server can be a challenge. You have to be able to read people, but you also have to get along well with the rest of the staff. This chapter will cover the basics of how to give great service for any shift and for every circumstance.

Anticipate Your Guests' Needs

You want to know what you guests need before they know it. It can be creepy to stalk your table, but part of giving great service is making sure your guests are taken care of.

Are they done?

You never want to just take someone's plate away before they're finished. Every server has had that angry customer that smacks their hand away and says, "Um, I wasn't done yet."

This will probably happen regardless of the telltale signs, but in general, the signs that a table is done eating include the following:

1. Placing a napkin on top of the plate
2. Pushing the plate to the side and turning the fork upside down across the plate
3. Both knife and fork placed together at an angle on the plate
4. Stacking plates

If you're really good at reading people, you also might notice if some time has passed and the guests have stopped eating. This may be a good time to ask if they want a box.

Regardless of the signs your table is putting off, you should always ask first before you start taking stuff of the table.

If you call a customer by their name, you can expect a higher tip to the tune of 10 percent.[13]

Fast Fact

Little things to just know

Here are 10 things you should always doing to deliver great service:

1. Serve hot food hot, on heated dishes.
2. Serve cold food chilled, on cold dishes.
3. Inquire how food is to be cooked:
    a. Eggs: fried or boiled, how many minutes.
    b. Steak: rare, medium, or well-done.
    c. Toast: buttered or dry.
4. Refill water glasses whenever necessary during the meal.
5. Serve extra butter when needed.
6. Refill coffee on request and according to management policies. Bring more cream if necessary.

7. Serve granulated sugar with fresh fruit and unsweetened iced drinks.
8. Place silver necessary for a course just prior to serving.
   a. Soup spoons on extreme right of teaspoons.
   b. Cocktail fork to right of soup spoon.
9. Offer crackers, toast, and other accompaniments or relishes with appetizer and soup courses, according to policies of management.
10. Place soda spoons and straws with malted milks, milkshakes and ice cream sodas.

Approaching the Table

You should approach a table within the first minute of customers being seated, looking professional and neat. Your shirt should be tucked in and ironed, and your apron should be clean. You should smile, make eye contact, and greet the customers, giving them your name. You, a busser, or the host should bring water to the table during or before this exchange.

Giving a friendly greeting

Efficient service alone will not win the customer's goodwill or make the person want to return. Every effort should be made to make the customer feel that everything possible will be done to satisfy his or her wants. To do this, you should greet the customer in a friendly, courteous manner and be interested and attentive when taking and serving the order.

Although a friendly attitude is important in relations with the customer, under no circumstances should personal matters be discussed with a customer. Your responsibility is to sell and to serve, not to entertain.

Squatting down at your table can help establish a social connection (and thus better tips) due to better eye contact and closer quarters. However, one study found that African-American customers tipped less when the server came too close. Professor Michael Lynn suspects that African-Americans prefer "having more personal space than whites and may have felt that a server squatting violated it."[14]

Giving prompt attention

Promptness in taking care of the customer is as important as greeting him or her in a friendly way. Just as the hostess should watch for the entrance of guests into the dining room, the server should closely observe her serving station and know when newly arrived guests are seated, and the counter server should be aware of the approach of customers wanting to be served.

The customer likes to be noticed, to be given a friendly greeting, and to have desirable seating. He or she has come to the restaurant for good food and service and expects his or her wants to be satisfied. Any special services, which the restaurant provides, that may be useful to the customer should be explained to him or her as the occasion arises. A few examples include:

1. A customer may want rapid service just before leaving on an early morning flight. When the restaurant has counter as well as table service, the customer should be told that he or she can be served more quickly if seated at the counter.

2. A mother may ask for an extra plate so that she may share her lunch with her child. When children's service is available with a special food selection, smaller portions, and lower prices, this service should be explained to her.

3. If a customer praises the hot homemade rolls, and the restaurant makes these available for take out orders, offer this service to the customer.

4. When a customer comments on the attractiveness of the courtyard, he or she may be told that dinners are served there under the trees during the summer months.

Drink orders

When you approach the table for the first time, you should ask if anyone would like a drink. You may want to make a suggestion or simply provide the customers with some information on what types of soft drinks, beers, or specialty cocktails the restaurant carries. Be sure you know drink jargon for this exchange; the guest who orders a vodka martini up with a twist will be upset if he or she receives a gin martini on the rocks! (See *Chapter 10: Understanding Alcohol* for all the common bar terminology.) This is also a good time to tell the table about any specials.

Give Great Table Service

Table service techniques will differ from restaurant to restaurant, but having a good foundation of the norm is a great skill to have under that belt of yours.

Here are some basic guidelines for serving from the left and the right:

1. Appetizers and salads should be served from the right with the right hand. The flatware for appetizers and salads is usually already on the table.

2. If soup is being served, make sure the bowl is on a plate. Soup spoons should be set to the right of the bowl and soup served from the right.

3. Entrées are also served from the right, placed so the main element of the plate faces the guest. Flatware for the entrée should be placed on the table before the entrée arrives. Be sure to only touch the flatware by the handle and plates by the rim. If side dishes are served on separate plates, they should be served from the left.

4. When serving dessert, you should place the utensil to the guest's left and serve the dessert from the right.

5. Drinks are served from the right, and coffee is poured from the right.

6. In general, all plates and other dishes should be cleared from the right.

7. Place and remove all food from the left side of the guest.

8. Place and remove all beverages, including water, from the right of the guest.

9. Use the left hand to place and remove dishes when working at the left side of the guest, and the right hand when working at the right side of the guest. This provides free arm action for you and avoids the danger of bumping against the guest's arm.

Here are some other things to keep in mind while giving table service:

1. Place each dish on the table, the four fingers of your left hand under the lower edge and your thumb on the upper edge of the plate.

2. Never reach in front of the guest, nor across one person in order to serve another.

3. Do not place soiled, chipped, or cracked glassware and china or bent or tarnished silverware before a guest.

4. Hold silverware by the handles when it is laid in place. Be sure it is clean and spotless.

5. Handle tumblers by their bases and goblets by their stems.

6. Set fruit juice and cocktail glasses, cereal dishes, soup bowls, and dessert dishes on small plates before placing them in the center of the cover, between the knife and the fork.

7. When it accompanies the main course, place the salad plate at the left of the forks, about two inches from the edge of the table. When the salad is served as a separate course, place it directly in front of the guest.

8. Place individual serving trays or bread and rolls above and to the left of the forks. Place a tray or basket of bread for the use of several guests toward the center of the table.

9. Place the cup and saucer at the right of the spoons, about two inches from the edge of the table. Turn the handle of the cup to the right, either parallel to the edge of the table or at a slight angle toward the guest.

10. Set tea and coffee pots on small plates and place above and slightly to the right of the beverage cup. Set iced beverage glasses on coasters or napkins to protect tabletops and linen.

11. Place individual creamers, syrup pitchers and small lemon plates above and a little to the right of the cup and saucer.

12. Place a milk glass at the right of and below the water glass.

13. Serve butter, cheese, and cut lemon with a fork. Serve relishes, pickles, and olives with a fork or spoon — not with the fingers.

More and more, food service operations are using booth- or banquet-type seating. It is extremely difficult to carry out proper table service in these situations.

The general rules for booth service are:

- Serve everything with the hand farthest from the guest; use your right hand to serve a guest at your left and your left hand to serve a guest to your right.

- Remove soiled plates with the hand nearest your guest while substituting the next course with the hand farthest from your guest.

You should also be trained on correct table settings. Generally, each member of the waitstaff is assigned to a group of tables. These sections are known as "stations."

You should provide tables that are properly set before service is given, with clean linen, polished silver, shining glassware and spotless china. Tables should be promptly cleared after service and reset as needed.

Domino's Pizza had to cancel their 30 minutes or less guarantee after so many drivers were getting into accidents while delivering pizzas.[15]

Fast Fact

Setting the table

The cover is the space — about 24 inches by 15 inches — within which one place is set with china, silver, linen, and glass. An imaginary line may be drawn defining this area to assist in laying the cover.

A silence pad, if used, should be placed evenly on the table so that the edges do not hang down below the tablecloth. The tablecloth is laid over the silence pad or undercover or directly over the table, with the center fold up and equidistant from the edges of the table. All four corners should fall an even distance from the floor. The cloth should be free from wrinkles, holes, and stains.

The folded napkin is placed at the left of the fork, with open corners at the lower right and about one inch from the front edge of the table.

Knives and forks should be laid about nine inches apart so that a dinner plate may be easily placed between them. The balance of the silverware is then placed to the right of the knife and to the left of the fork in the order in which it is to be used (placing the first-used at the outside and proceeding toward the plate).

The handles of all silver should be perpendicular to the table edge and about one inch from the edge. Forks are placed at the left side of the cover, tines pointed up. Knives are placed at the right side of the cover with the cutting edge turned toward the plate. Spoons are laid, bowls up, at the right of the knives.

Oyster and cocktail forks are placed at the extreme right of the cover beyond the teaspoons or laid across the right side of the service plate underlying the cocktail glass or the oyster service.

Breakfast or luncheon forks, salad forks, and dessert forks are placed next to the plate in order of use; the spoons are arranged to the right of the forks, in order of use, beginning in each instance with the first course (on the outside) and working toward the center of the cover. When knives are not used in the cover, both the forks and spoons are placed to the right of the cover.

The bread-and-butter plate is placed at the left of the cover, directly above the tines of the meat fork. The water glass is placed at the right of the cover, immediately above the point of the dinner knife.

Wine, liquor, and beer glasses, if applicable, are placed to the right of the water glass.

Salt and pepper shakers are generally placed in the center of small tables. When wall tables for two are set, the shakers usually are placed on the side nearest the wall or the side nearest the room rather than in the center of the table.

When a large table is being set up and several sets of sugars and creamers are needed, the cream pitchers and sugar bowls may be placed at equal distances down the center of the table. Guests can more conveniently handle them if the handles are turned toward the cover. When several sets of salt and pepper shakers are used on a large table, they may be placed between the covers on a line parallel with the bases of the water glasses.

Folding napkins

The fold of napkins in an establishment is important in setting the ambiance. Usually more casual establishments will use simpler folds, and fine-dining venues will use more elaborate folding techniques. Make sure you begin with clean, ironed napkins. Learn from your trainer how to properly fold the napkins, and make sure you take your time with this. A sloppy place setting can set the wrong mood for your guests.

Centerpieces

Whatever type of centerpiece is used, you must learn how to maintain the centerpieces. If using fresh flowers, change the flowers whenever they start to look wilted. Silk and dried flowers will need to be kept free of dust, as will candles and any other object used in the centerpiece, such as a basket or vase. Candles should also be replaced frequently so they look clean and fresh.

Here are some other things to keep in mind:

- Napkins should be folded carefully according to the style of the restaurant, with folds straight and edges even.

- Menus always must be replaced with new ones if they become soiled or torn.

- Flowers should be arranged in containers appropriate in color, size, and shape.

- Individual creamers should be washed and thoroughly cooled before being filled with cream. A container with a slender spout is used for filling if a cream dispenser is not available. Care should be taken not to fill creamers too full.

- Serving trays should be kept clean and dry to protect both the your uniform and the serving-table surface. The top of the tray should be wiped clean before it is loaded to prevent the bottoms of the dishes from being soiled.

- Ice cubes should be clean. Ice should be transported in containers for ice only. Ice should be considered a food item.

- Chairs and booths should have crumbs dusted off after each guest has left. Backs, rounds and legs of chairs should be carefully dusted every day.

- Silver or stainless should be cleaned according to the special directions of the restaurant. When a cream polish is used, it should be rubbed with a soft cloth or a small brush over the surface and well into the embossed pattern of the silverware. The silver should then be thoroughly washed, rinsed and polished with a dry cloth to remove all traces of the silver cream.

Almost a third of America's food dollar is spent on dining out services.[16]

Breakfast Service

Good breakfast service is important because many customers are in a hurry, some aren't that hungry, and some are just nasty people until they've had their coffee. A cheerful attitude on your part as well as prompt and efficient service will help customers start the day on the right foot.

Foods served for breakfast are most palatable when they are freshly prepared and when they're served at the correct temperature. The waitperson, therefore, should serve breakfast in courses unless the customer especially requests that the whole order be served at once. Cooked foods and hot beverages should be brought to the customer directly from the serving station and under no circumstances allowed to remain on the serving stand to cool while the customer finishes a preceding course.

Order of breakfast service

1. When fresh fruit or fruit juice is ordered, serve it first and then remove the soiled dishes before placing the toast and coffee.

2. When customers order a combination of cooked fruit, toast, and coffee, they may ask to have the whole order served at once. Place the fruit dish in the center of the cover, the plate of toast at the left of the forks, and the coffee at the right of the teaspoons.

3. When the breakfast order includes a cereal and a hot dish, the service procedure may be as follows:

   a. Place the fruit course in the center of the cover.
   b. Remove the fruit service.
   c. Place the cereal bowl in the center of the cover. Cut individual boxes of cereal partway through the side near the top so the guest may open them easily.
   d. Remove the cereal service.
   e. Place the breakfast plate of eggs, meat, or other hot food in the center of the cover. Place the plate of toast at the left of the forks. Place the coffee service at the right of the spoons.

f. Remove the breakfast plate and the bread plate.

g. Place the sales check, face down, at the right of the cover or present it on a clean change tray.

Lunch Service

Lunch customers can usually be classified in two groups: businesspeople who have a short lunch period and want quick service, and shoppers and hostess groups who want more leisurely service. Your job is to avoid keeping customers in the first group waiting for service, and to avoid making those in the second group feel like they're being rushed.

Order of lunch service

1. Fill the water glasses three-fourths full of iced water.
2. Place chilled butter on a cold bread-and-butter plate.
3. Place the appetizer in the center of the cover.

4. Remove the appetizer when the guest has finished.

5. Place the soup service in the center of the cover.

6. Remove the soup.

7. Place the entrée plate in center of cover.

8. If salad is served with the main course, place the salad at the left of the forks, about two inches from edge of table.

9. Place tray or basket of bread and rolls at the left of the salad plate.

10. Place hot beverages above and a little to the right of the cup and saucer, with individual creamer above the cup.

11. Place an iced beverage or milk at the right and a little below the water glass.

12. Remove the main-course dishes.

13. Remove any extra silver not used for the main course.

14. Place dessert silver to the right of the cover, with fork nearest the dessert plate, if fork and teaspoon are used. When several teaspoons are placed, the dessert fork may be laid on the left side, to "balance the cover."

15. Place the dessert service in center of the cover.

16. Serve hot coffee if requested.

17. Remove dessert dishes and silver.

18. Present the check face down.

Fast Fact

Wear something different. Servers who individualized themselves with a flower in their hair or a trendy bowtie earned over $1 more per customer in tips.[17]

Dinner Service

Because dinner guests are seldom in a hurry, you are able to give them a more leisurely type of service. Although the guest should be allowed plenty of time to complete each course, long waits between courses should be avoided. You should watch the guests during the meal in order to serve the next course promptly.

Order of dinner service

1. From the left, place the appetizer in the center of the cover.
2. Remove the first-course dishes.
3. Place the soup in the center of the cover.
4. Remove the soup.
5. Place the entrée in the center of the cover.
6. Place salad at the left of the forks when it is served with the main course.
7. Place beverages to the right of teaspoons.
8. Offer rolls or place them to the left of the salad plate.
9. Remove the main-course dishes when the guest has finished.
10. Place silver for the dessert course.
11. Place the dessert in the center of the cover.
12. Serve hot coffee.

Carrying Trays

Carrying trays is a large part of your job, and there are right and wrong ways to go about it. There are several things you will want to keep in mind when dealing with trays.

If you are carrying a large tray, you should set it down on a tray jack to serve. It is easy enough to serve from a small tray, but serving becomes a hazard if you try to hold a heavy tray and serve from it. Another option is to have a second server tail you and hold the tray while you serve from it.

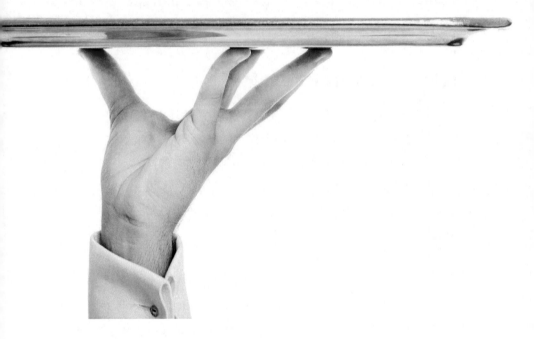

Loading trays

Load food trays with the heaviest entrée nearest to your body so that you can use your body to help balance. Also be sure you are balancing the entrées on the tray. Plates that are going out to the dining room should never be stacked; if you need two trays, use two trays.

When you load your tray, put the larger, heavier dinner plates and dishes in the center, and the lighter pieces toward the edges. Hot and cold dishes do not touch. Tea and coffee pots are not filled so full that liquid will leak from the spouts. Pot spouts are turned in and away from plates or food. A tray should be loaded so that it will be evenly balanced and the objects on it will neither slip nor spill while it is being carried. Among the precautions to take in loading a tray are the following:

- Before leaving a serving station, check the order to see that it is correct, complete, properly cooked, the right quantity for serving, properly garnished and attractively served, with no spilled food on the edges of dishes.
- Before leaving the kitchen, check to see that all food and the necessary serving equipment for the course are on the tray.
- Check that the tray is clean.
- Load heavier items in the center of the tray.
- Don't overload the tray.
- If carrying a large tray, set it down on a tray jack to serve.
- Handles should face outward so that the server can easily grasp the cup or glass.
- If carrying food or drinks without trays, only do it for small parties so that all the food can go out at once.

More than nine out of 10 restaurant employees age 35 and older advance to a higher paying job in the industry.[18]

Fast Fact

Cocktail trays

Cocktail trays should be loaded with the heaviest drink in the center to balance the tray. Handles should face outward so that you can easily grasp the cup or glass.

Arm service

Many servers carry food or drinks without trays. This should only be done for small parties so that all the food can go out at once. If the party is large enough to require two trips using arm service, you should use a tray.

Bussing

When using trays for bussing, make sure that you stack "like" plates in neat stacks. You should do this as quietly as possible in the dining room. Furthermore, don't scrape the plates while still in the dining room; this is unappetizing and can easily be done in the back.

Taking Care of Children

Think back to when you were a kid. Where was your favorite place to eat? It probably had less to do with the food than it did with the atmosphere, the toys that came with the meal, the playground outside, or the games and coloring books on the table.

More and more restaurant owners are realizing the importance of kid-appeal and how it affects where a family decides to eat. Not every restaurant necessarily needs a jungle gym, but children tell their parents when they enjoy a restaurant, and this is as good as a five-star review.

Keep them occupied

If your restaurant has crayons or games on hand, give them to kids to keep them occupied until the food is served.

If your restaurant allows, bring items such as desserts to the table for preparation and offer an array of favorite sprinkles for their ice cream or whipped cream.

Talk to the kids as well as the adults. Granted, you aren't a baby-sitter, but anything you can do to help the parents and entertain the kids will be welcomed by your guests. You should also be familiar with the kids' menu so you can make suggestions and answer any questions the kids might have.

Paying attention to kids not only helps their parents, but it helps your other customers as well, since an occupied child is less likely to be a screaming child.

Speedy service

Make sure you serve children's drinks and something to munch on, as quickly as possible, if it looks like the order may take a little while. Granted, you aren't a babysitter, but anything you can do to help the parents have a relaxing meal and to entertain the kids will be welcomed by your guests with children. Paying attention to kids also helps your other customers, since an occupied child is less likely to be a screaming child!

If you have a bad attitude towards children, the parents and the children will probably feel uncomfortable during the meal and — worst of all— won't tip well! But, if you treat kids as human beings and not merely something to be dealt with, you'll surely please your guests and have a better chance of earning a good tip.

Fast Fact

Research from the National Restaurant Association found that one of the top trends for restaurant menus in 2016 was healthier options for kids.

Keep an eye out for messes

Kids can be chaotic eaters no matter how old they are. Be sure to check on family tables often so you can help clean up any accidental spills or messes.

CASE STUDY:
Kelly Meister-Yetter

Freelance writer
Waited tables for 15 years;
started serving at age 21

I waited tables for over 10 years, and the No. 1 thing restaurants fail to properly teach is customer service. Customer service involves knowing the menu you're serving, so if someone asks how a dish is prepared, you don't have to look like an amateur by running to the kitchen each time the guest asks a question.

Be attentive — check in with your guest a few minutes after you've served them, and again two or three more times to ensure that everything is as it should be. If there's a problem, deal with it immediately, courteously, and professionally. If you can get away with giving a guest a free dessert (or if management doesn't offer) after a guest experienced a problem with the meal, then do it.

Don't ask "is that all for you today?" Ask "are you ready for coffee?" Don't ask if they want dessert; bring them the dessert tray. Finally, and probably most important, if you know that something on the menu is below par, then tell your guest that you don't recommend it, and suggest something else. It's better to stave off a problem than to have to deal with something you could've avoided by being honest with the customer.

Worst restaurant experience: I waited on a party of 10 and everything was going fine. I served them drinks, took their orders, and brought their salads. It was after I served the salads that the cook — one of the worst I'd ever worked with — told me that he was out of NY strips. Four people in the party had ordered NY strips! Dismayed, I hurried to the table, explained the shortage, hurried back to the kitchen, and told the cook. I assumed he would rush those last four orders, but he didn't (and the restaurant wasn't even busy at the time!). About the time the other six were finishing their dinners, I was just serving the four. The party was deeply unhappy, and I didn't blame them one bit. They thought it was my fault, though — not the fault of the kitchen. So, I ended up embarrassed, really mad at the cook, and with a crummy tip to boot! After that, I always made that cook inventory his stock *before* I took any orders!

Best restaurant experience (for the sheer novelty of it): I was working the breakfast/lunch shift one Sunday at a Sheraton. They did a brunch on Sundays that was very popular with the older folks who would come and fill the place up for a few hours. This particular morning, the hostess seated five men in my section. They looked a whole lot different without make-up, but I recognized the band Kiss and their manager all the same. And while their behavior was subdued (they spent their time quietly eating and reading newspapers), the wild hair alone was enough to make the old folks around them a little nervous! They had no idea who the men were, of course — they just knew that some very strange-looking men had invaded the restaurant!

Kelly Meister-Yetter is an author who spent 10 years supplementing her income by waiting tables in fine dining establishments.

13. Shin, 2014.
14. Shin, 2014.
15. Janofsky, 1993.
16. US Department of Agriculture, 2016.
17. Shin, 2014.
18. National Restaurant Association, 2016.

Chapter 5

Taking
Orders

Taking the order is arguably the most important part of waiting tables. This single interaction can make for a pleasant experience for all, or it can be the beginning to a horrible spiral down the rabbit hole. This information can easily be learned by shadowing other waitstaff. Here are some useful guidelines for you to follow.

Customers usually like to have time to study the menu without feeling that their waiter is waiting impatiently to take their order. You should be ready to attend to your guests as soon as they're ready. This is where your awkward stalking comes into play. Look for the following signs to know if your table is ready:

- The menus are closed
- The menus are stacked at the edge of the table
- You feel they are looking at you for extended lengths of time
- They are waving their hands at you

This can be really awkward, but look for these signs so that you don't unintentionally bother your table or make them feel rushed. It's also a good idea to stop by after a few minutes regardless of the signs because many people don't really understand the universal sign of closing the menu to signal to the waiter that you're ready to order.

When they're finally ready to order, you should stand close enough to hear your table easily and to answer questions distinctly. When you write the order, you should write legibly, use correct abbreviations, and indicate the number of guests and table number.

While taking the order, you should ask for all the information you need to serve the meal satisfactorily. For example:

- What kind of dressing is preferred for the salad?
- How would you like the steak cooked?
- Are you OK with the onions on the dish?

It's always a good idea to make sure the guest wants every ingredient in the dish. You shouldn't go through the entire list, but pick out the ones that many often ask to be removed, such as onions, olives, tomatoes, and the like. There's always that one table that orders the cheeseburger and asks for a remake because they didn't realize it came with mustard on it.

Fast Fact

Complimenting your customer's food order can earn you some extra cash. In various tests, the average tip rose around 2-3 percent when the server said something like, "You all made good choices!" or "Nice choice!"[19]

Giving and Collecting Orders

The procedures used for giving and collecting orders in the kitchen vary somewhat with different restaurants. However, certain general methods help to determine the speed of the service as well as the condition of the food when it is placed before the customer. When you, as the waiter, are courteous and considerate in giving and assembling your order, you help to maintain a good relationship between the kitchen and dining room personnel.

You should not make a habit of saying you are in a hurry for your orders; the cooks are probably doing their best to fill orders quickly and in rotation. When extra-fast service is really necessary, you may be justified in asking to be served rapidly or even out of turn.

Timing the order

If your table orders appetizers, the main meal, and dessert all at one time, you should space out your ordering. Often times, the restaurant you work at will have specific guidelines about this, but in general, customers expect you to handle the timing of their meal appropriately. A basic rule of thumb is to wait until the food hits the table before ringing in the next course.

Explaining the menu

You should be familiar with the menu contents, its arrangement, and its prices. To illustrate:

1. New customers are often confused as to where to find certain items on the unfamiliar menu. You should be quick to offer requested assistance in finding what the customer wants.

2. Sometimes the customer fails to notice specials or some other featured group of foods on the menu. You may point these out to the customer.

3. A foreign name or an unfamiliar term on the menu may be confusing to the reader. A simple explanation of the meaning of the term or a description of the dish will be appreciated. The server should give such explanations with an attitude of helpfulness.

4. A customer with poor eyesight may have difficulty in reading the menu. The server could read the items to him and write his order.

Taking the food order

If there are children at the table, you may want to start with them. Take clues from the table. If one woman is obviously undecided, you may make her uncomfortable by insisting she places her order first. Let the others order, then come back to her. Make sure you know the menu and can answer any questions about menu item preparation. If the customer asks or seems unsure, you may also make recommendations at this point.

Delivering the food

Make sure you know that food is served from the right side of the guest and plates are cleared from the right. Also, be sure that when you hold plates that you are only touching them on the edge. It's gross to see your server's thumb in your mashed potatoes! Additionally, you should bring everyone's food at the same time. Make sure to warn guests when plates are hot.

Checking back

Be sure to check back with guests within the first two to three minutes of being served. If there is a problem, you will be able to take care of it immediately. Don't let the customer sit stewing about their cold stew. Pun intended.

Touching customers has been proven to increase sales, store ratings, and tips. In one study, customers that weren't touched left a 12 percent tip while those who were touched twice tipped 17 percent.[20]

Dessert

When you are clearing the entrée plates or not long after, you should ask if the table wants desserts, coffees or after-dinner drinks. If your restaurant has them, offer your customers dessert menus. You could also make suggestions for desserts to split if everyone is feeling quite full. Often, a table will split a dessert, and one sale is better than none!

Presenting the check

The guest should not be kept waiting for the check. It should be presented as soon as he or she has finished eating. The check should be correctly totaled and laid face down on the table. When a group of several people has been served, the check should be placed by the person who is in charge; if you don't know who that is, the check should be placed toward the center of the table.

It is a good idea to ask if your customer needs anything else before presenting the check and to thank the customer as the check is laid on the table. When a credit card is presented, be sure to include a pen and the appropriate instruction, such as, "The top white copy is yours, and the bottom yellow copy is for the restaurant." When paying in cash, you should leave the appropriate change, and make sure you've supplied the right kinds of bills to warrant a tip. For example, if someone's change is $10, you might want to give them two fives and five ones instead of a single 10 dollar bill.

Change should be placed on a change tray or tip tray provided for that purpose. Do not indicate in any way that a tip is expected or that any certain amount is anticipated. It is also inappropriate to show disappointment because the tip was less than expected.

When it looks obvious that the table is getting ready to go or when the customer asks for the check, you should bring it promptly. It's also a good idea for you to explain the restaurant's payment procedures, as some customers will wonder if they go up front to pay or if they pay you. You could say, "When you're ready, I'll come back to take care of that for you."

It's a nice touch to say goodbye as the party is leaving. It leaves the customer with a friendly feeling. After all, they've just spent an hour or so in your company! This sort of courtesy makes customers feel that they have been truly welcomed guests.

Serving Multiple Tables

Once you master how to wait on one table, you need to learn how to wait on multiple tables. Let's say you are responsible for three tables. The first two tables are seated at the same time. You bring water to both of these tables. Then, you should take a drink order from each table. By the time you return with the drinks, the host has seated the third table. You should stay with the first two tables and see if they're ready to order. If they are, you should then take the order. Then, swing by and get a drink order from Table 3. Next, you should take the food order from Tables 1 and 2 to the kitchen. After you drop this off, you should return with Table 3's beverages and see if they are ready to order.

General Tips for Serving Customers

Approach the table

- Smile and warmly greet the customer.
- Introduce yourself and be courteous.

Get guests settled

- Help with any additional seating such as highchairs and booster chairs.
- Remove extra place settings.
- Help any guests with disabilities.
- Present guests with menus from the right side using your right hand.

Take drink order

- Ask guests if they would like to start with a drink.
- Make sure to get all the details of drink orders, such as whether guests want their drink on the rocks or up, and check on garnishes.
- Pay special attention to children, getting their drink order, and seeing if the customer would like for the children to be served right away.

Serve drinks

- Place a beverage napkin in front of the guest.
- Serve all drinks from the right and place on the beverage napkin.

Tell about specials

- When you bring the initial drink order, tell the guests about any specials, describing preparation methods, ingredients, and price.

Check back for second drink order and appetizer order

- If second drinks are ordered, remove the first glasses and napkins.
- Ask the guests if they have any questions about the menu or specials.
- Ask if guests would like an appetizer or salad to start their meals.

Flynn McGarry, a 16-year-old prodigal chef, is among the youngest in the world to open up a restaurant. McGarry went from preparing an eight-course tasting menu for guests in his living room to serving up classic American cuisine at $160-a-head. McGarry's Eureka is located in New York City's posh West Village neighborhood.[21]

Take food order

- Ask guests if they are ready to order. Take orders if they are.
- Suggest salads or side dishes that might be appropriate with entrée selections.
- Make sure to collect all the information you need, such as doneness of meat selections and choice of side dishes.
- Use correct abbreviations when filling out the guest checks.

- When taking the order, be sure to move around the table so you can speak to each guest one on one.
- Continue to take the orders in a clockwise pattern around the table.
- Collect the menus.
- Tidy up the table as needed.

Meeting special requests

- Make sure you know the menu and are able to suggest alternatives to guests with allergies and dietary restrictions, etc.

- Write all special requests on your guest check clearly, and make sure to communicate the information to the cooks verbally as well.

- Check with kitchen staff on ingredient questions and to ensure that particular substitutions can be made.

Deliver salads and appetizers

- Provide extra plates if guests are sharing an appetizer plate.
- Provide any sauces that come with appetizers.

Serving food and picking up food

- Collect all the needed serving equipment and cold accompaniments, such as bread, crackers, butter and cream.

- Pick up cold foods next, taking care to keep them away from hot food on the tray.

- The hot food should be picked up last.

- If hot breads are served, pick them up last to serve them in their best condition.

- Rinse tea and coffee pots with hot water before filling them with hot beverages. Never pour iced drinks into warm glasses or place butter on a warm plate.

- While waiting for the orders, be sure to check back with table to see if they need drinks or anything else.

- If an order is taking longer than you expected, check with the head chef or kitchen manager about the delay.

- If food is delayed, do not let guests wait with no explanation. If the manager approves and the delay is significant, you can offer the guests a free beverage or appetizer as you apologize for the delay.

- If you are too busy to pick up an order when it is ready, seek assistance from another server, a bus person, the host or hostess, or manager.

- Check all orders before delivering them to the table to ensure they are correct.

- Make sure plates are attractive (with no smudges or splattered sauces), all garnishes are on the plates, and the temperature is correct (hot foods are hot and cold foods are cold).

Preparing the table for serving and clearing dishes

- Place steak knives at the guests' place settings, if needed.

- Bring any condiments the guests might need, making sure the bottles are full.

- Check with guests to see if they would like another beverage with their meal.

- After any course, dishes should be removed from the left side, except beverages, which should be removed from the right.

Delivering food

- Use a tray to carry more than two entrées.
- Serve children first.
- Serve food from the guest's left with your left hand when possible, but don't reach over customers.
- Place the entrée plate so the main item is closest to the customer.
- Place side dishes to the left of the entrée plate.

- Ask guests if they need anything else.
- Remove dirty plates from previous courses as well as empty glasses.

Fast Fact

The world's most expensive hamburger can be found in Las Vegas at a restaurant called Fleur. It will cost you $5,000.[22]

Dessert

- When clearing dinner dishes, ask if guests would like coffee and/or if they would like to see the dessert menu.
- Be ready to describe desserts to guests, and suggest that they might want to share a dessert.

- Bring coffee orders with cream and sugar.
- Bring dessert orders (with extra plates and forks if guests are sharing).
- Bring coffee refills.

Clearing the table

- Platters and other serving dishes should be removed first when clearing the table, or they may be removed as soon as empty.

- The main-course plate should be removed first, the salad plate next followed by the bread-and-butter plate.

- The empty beverage glass is removed from the right after the main course.

- The table should be crumbed by using a small plate and a clean, folded napkin. This is especially important when hard rolls or crusty breads are served.

- Hot tea and coffee should be left on the table until the dessert course is finished.

- The water glass should remain on the table and be kept refilled as long as the guest is seated.

- When a guest is seated at a table and it is necessary to change a soiled tablecloth, turn the soiled cloth halfway back, lay the clean cloth half open in front of the guest, and transfer the tableware to the clean cloth. The soiled cloth may then be drawn from the table and the clean one pulled smoothly into place. Soiled linen should be properly disposed of immediately after it is removed from the table.

Paying the check

- Present the bill in a guest check folder, and tell the guest you will take it when they are ready.
- Resolve any questions or discrepancies on the bill.
- If the guest is paying with cash, present the change in a guest check folder.
- Don't take the tip from the table until the guest leaves.
- If the guest is using a credit card, run the credit card for approval. If the card is declined, politely ask the guest for another card or if they would prefer to pay in cash. When returning after the approval has cleared, make sure to bring a pen for the guest's convenience. Also make sure the guest has signed the credit card receipt and left the restaurant's copy.
- Thank the guest when returning with the receipt and/or change, and invite them back.
- Inform management or security if a guest leaves without paying.

CASE STUDY:
Katy Kassian

Small business speaker,
consultant, advocate, and writer
Waited tables for 33 years,
started at the age of 14

I'm an "old school" vet of waitressing. I started slinging hash at 14. The best advice I can give to new servers is:

1. Don't take it personally. Ever.

2. Listen. "Professional eavesdropping," as some of the older-than-me timers called it, pays off. Knowing who has what and being able to help someone else helps you.

3. No matter what some guy says, don't take it personally. Especially if you work in a truck stop or café environment. Odds are good that he says that to every waitress, everywhere. It's not personal. Same as most crabby customers — they are just that way. It's not you.

4. Make the most of it.

I managed to travel coast to coast, attended all of my kids' sports and events, paid for my house, and had more personal freedom waitressing then I ever would have in most other "regular" jobs. The perks far outweigh the cons. There is always someone who needs a day off to leave early, which frees up extra hours for you if you want them. It's easy enough to swap shifts, too.

Worst restaurant experience: I was working the counter and a man stood up from eating and was dead before he hit the floor. Yes. Really. Talk about ruining a good day. The ensuing drama was pretty epic for us, too. The family of the gentleman tried to sue the restaurant stating that if we hadn't "let" him eat bacon that day, then he would still be alive. (I'm pretty sure that was NOT the case!)

Best restaurant experience: Boy-o! There's been so many good experiences. One of my favorites was working a truck stop in Colorado, and a driver couldn't get home for Christmas, so we all pitched in to get him a plane ticket.

I started waitressing at 14 in my uncle's café in Sacramento. They were shorthanded and called the house to see if I would fill in. I was given a book, pointed at the counter, and told, "Learn or don't come back!" Talk about trial by fire! I stuck with waitressing for 33 years. Through college, kids, marriages, and many states, it has never let me down. You couldn't ask for a better industry to be a part of. The camaraderie is like no other. And the skills you will learn will take you anywhere in life. I have translated many of them into my current position as a speaker on small business and rural communities.

19. Shin, 2014.
20. Shin, 2014.
21. Chocano, 2014.
22. Mealey, 2016.

Chapter 6

Suggestive Selling

C ustomers might want information about the menu or suggestions
about the food selection before
deciding on their order. If you're well informed
and intelligent, you can be of real service to the
guest while also merchandising food effectively for
the restaurant. This is an opportunity to be more
than an order-taker; you can be a successful sales-
person as well.

Before you are ready to take an order intelligently,
you must study the menu and be familiar with the
day's specials and the choices of foods offered on

the selective menu. When a foreign name or an uncommon term is used in describing any product, you should be able to pronounce the name correctly and to know what it means in terms of the method of preparation or the manner of service. Some guest is sure to ask for such information about the product. It's annoying to the guest if you can't answer promptly and have to go find someone else who knows the answer.

Plus, it will help you in the tip department if you come across as knowledgeable even if you're completely bluffing your way through the description of the étouffée.

Food and drink sales in the United States' restaurant industry reached $42.8 billion in 1970. Today, these sales are over $745 billion.[23]

Suggesting Selections to the Customer

When a customer is unfamiliar with the restaurant, is hesitant about his food choice, or is confused about where to find certain items on the menu, you have a real opportunity to be helpful by offering suitable suggestions. The server should be tactful in offering these suggestions and should use intelligence about their form and timing. For example:

- A vegetable plate or a salad and sandwich combination may be suggested when a guest says that she "wants something light."

- The "mixed grill special" may be suggested to a guest who can't find a meat that appeals to him on the regular dinner menu.

- You may suggest that "the fried chicken is very nice" or "the baked ham is especially good" to an uncertain diner who is having difficulty making a selection.

- You should be able to assist the customer, if necessary, to improve the nutritional value and taste of the meal. You may suggest a fresh vegetable or a salad when a man orders a meat and potato combination, or recommend a sherbet or fresh fruit rather than a rich dessert when a customer has had roast pork for the main course and asks the server to suggest a dessert.

- The guest may be tempted by the roast lamb offered on the menu, but feels that he cannot afford to pay so much. The server may suggest that roast lamb also is available on a "dinner special" without a first course or dessert, at a lesser price.

Tact and discretion must be used when making suggestions to customers. The customer should feel that he or she is being favored by the suggestion and not being forced to buy. When your suggestion is not accepted by the guest, you should in no way show annoyance or disappointment.

The guest may be influenced to give a more complete order than he or she would otherwise through your suggestions. For instance:

- When the customer orders a sandwich or a salad, you may ask, "Which do you prefer to drink: tea, coffee, or milk?" and influence the customer to add a beverage to his original order.

- When the customer orders a grilled food that must be cooked to order, tell the customer the time required and then ask if he or she would like an appetizer or a soup.

- When an a la carte order for a meat course has been served, you may return to the table, present the opened menu and ask, "Would you like to select a dessert?" Another form of suggestion is to name an attractive dessert such as, "The chocolate pie is very good," or "We have fresh peach ice cream today."

Making Substitutions

Should the guest ask for a substitution on the regular menu, a half-portion or a special service, you should make sure that such service is permitted before promising it. If there is any doubt about the matter, it should be referred to the manager for decision.

Purposes of Suggestive Selling

Restaurant customers may be grouped into two categories:

1. Those who know what they want to order
2. Those who have no idea

Indecision may be due to unfamiliarity with the restaurant, difficulty in interpreting the menu, a lack of appetite, or a limited budget. In each case, you can help the customer, either by giving information or by making suggestions.

Whenever you prompt a customer to order something that he or she probably would not have ordered otherwise, you are using suggestive salesmanship.

Meeting the Needs of the Customer

The best kind of suggestive selling is that which is based on knowledge of the customer's likes and dislikes. This type of selling is particularly applicable to the regular customer. You should try to learn the customer's preferences in order to make suggestions that will be pleasing.

For example, you may suggest an oyster stew to a tired, chilled motorist; a warm meal to a hungry industrial worker; a salad and sandwich plate to a shopper. When the restaurant is located near the sea, you may suggest seafood to travelers. The suggestion of foods that are typical of any geographical region is usually appreciated by the visitor to the region.

You should consider the amount the customer wishes to pay when making suggestions about food selection. You should try to adapt suggestions to the general price level the customer can afford in order to complete a sale that will probably be satisfactory.

If the customer signifies that he is willing to spend $20 for his dinner, then an effort should be made to sell him a meal at that price. On the other hand, if the customer indicates that he wishes to limit his expenditure to $10 or less, you should help him find a satisfactory selection at that price.

You may make suggestions that will help the customer to meet his nutritional requirements. When the customer tells you about his dietary restrictions or asks for suggestions for a well-balanced meal, you may suggest articles of food and combinations on the menu that best meet his needs. For example:

- Suggest fresh fruit when sweet desserts are banned or sugar is rationed.

- Suggest French dressing instead of mayonnaise, or ice cream instead of custard, when eggs are not allowed.

- Suggest broth soup instead of cream soup and roast chicken in place of chicken a la king, when the customer has a dairy allergy.

- When wheat products are eliminated from the customer's diet, you should carefully avoid serving meat with gravy, except natural, unthickened meat juice, and should substitute rye wafers or bread for wheat-flour breads, and a baked apple, a fruit sherbet, or a dish of fresh fruit for the pie or cake on the menu.

- When the customer is counting calories, you may be helpful by suggesting low-calorie foods that are appealing.

One third of Americans got their first job experience in a restaurant.[24]

Fast Fact

Upselling Items

You may suggest additional items to the customer, which increase the size of the order. The purpose of upselling is to help the customer make a satisfactory selection while also increasing your tip. This type of suggestive selling may be used to advantage when the customer is ordering from an a la carte menu. For instance:

- Suggest a beverage with an order for a salad or dessert.
- Suggest a sandwich with an order for a soup or a milkshake.
- Suggest a soup, cocktail, or some other "beginner" with an order for grilled or fried food that must be cooked to order.
- Suggest a vegetable or a salad with an order for meat and potatoes.
- A customer who has ordered a main course combination that does not include dessert may be encouraged to order dessert;

for example, "We have fresh Georgia peach shortcake today," or "The Colorado cantaloupe is very good." The presentation of the menu and the inquiry, "What would you like for dessert?" may initiate a sale, whereas the question, "Would you like something else?" will probably not.

Promoting Specials

Before you can suggest a special, you must be familiar with what the special is. Ask your chef or manager for a detailed description before the shift begins; perhaps they could even offer a tasting so you can better describe the special to the customers.

Restaurants offer specials for various reasons. Focus on these reasons when selling them to your customers:

- Specials are made from local ingredients.
- Specials are made from seasonal ingredients.
- Specials offer a better price value.
- Specials are smaller portions.

- Specials are items that aren't usually on the menu.
- Specials are items the restaurant is trying out before putting on the menu.

Suggesting Higher-Priced Items

The food or menu suggested by the server may be more expensive than the one the customer otherwise would have chosen. In this case, as when suggesting additional items, you should consider the customer's desires and satisfaction more important than the amount of the sale. You may suggest higher-priced items when something like the following happens: The customer is uncertain about his selection, and remarks that a chicken sandwich is all he sees that appeals to him. You could suggest that the customer might enjoy a club sandwich made with chicken and go on to describe how it's made. If this suggestion results in the sale of the club sandwich, the size of the check is increased, and the customer may be better nourished as well as better pleased because he has had a well-planned dinner.

Timing of Suggestions

Menu suggestions should be made at an appropriate time. For example:

- Make suggestions for the meal selection when the customer is undecided about his initial choice or gives an order for an incomplete course or meal.

- Suggest a dessert just before the customer finishes the main course. At a cafeteria serving counter, you may suggest articles of food displayed at any section of the counter.

Suggestions should be positive rather than negative. When asked the question, "Will that be all?" just as he has completed the main course, a customer will ordinarily reply, "Yes." "Would you like to order a dessert now?" on the other hand, is positive and will likely be answered in the affirmative.

When an article that has been chosen is "out," you should know that the supply is exhausted, explain the shortage to the customer, and suggest something else that may be equally pleasing. First, however, you must try to overcome the guest's disappointment that the article he chose is not available. By expressing regret that there are no fresh strawberries left, and by suggesting that the fresh raspberries are delicious, you may succeed in selling a substitute and in maintaining the customer's goodwill.

Success in suggestive selling depends to a large degree upon the interest you show when making the suggestion to the customer and the enthusiasm you express for the quality of the suggested product.

The number of restaurants owned by women has increased by more than 40 percent since 2007.[25]

Value-Added Service

There are certain behaviors you should engage in to provide good service, and then there are behaviors that transform adequate service into value-added service. Try following these guidelines to increase your tips!

Make recommendations

If, for instance, a customer can't decide on an entrée or a wine, make sure you offer recommendations. For example, you could say, "I tried the halibut special, and it was delicious!" Making suggestions can be very intuitive. Look for clues about what type of dining experience the patrons are after. Does it seem like a special occasion? If so, customers are more likely to order appetizers and desserts. Do they seem to be on a budget? Then suggest a mid- or lower-priced entrée. Remember, these are all suggestions; don't get pushy.

Remember guests' likes and dislikes

Everyone likes to be remembered. If you have regular customers, try to remember their specific food likes and dislikes. For example, if a couple comes in and always orders the same wine, have it ready for them next time before they ask for it. It's guaranteed to charm. It's likely that if they were going to order something different that evening, they will take "the usual" because they appreciate you remembering their preference.

Be willing to customize

If a customer asks for the steak without sauce, say "No problem!" If the customer wants to substitute rice for potatoes, do so without making a big fuss.

Suggest alternatives

If the kitchen has sold out of a particular dish, or if dietary restrictions do not allow a patron to order a particular dish, you should offer alternatives. If, for example there is a dairy product in the mashed potatoes and the guest is lactose intolerant, you could suggest, "Our roasted potatoes are made with olive oil; perhaps you would like to substitute those?"

Single diners

Single diners are often uncomfortable dining out. You might add to this discomfort by ignoring them. Make sure you pay attention to these single diners. Lone diners, however, often turn out to be businesspeople who are using expense accounts, so the sales and tip potential are high. If the guest seems to want to be left alone, seat him or her in a secluded part of the dining room. If they seem eager to talk, spend a moment chatting.

Reinforce a guest's choice

A couple decides to order a bottle of Merlot and are choosing between wine A and wine B. Compliment their decision. Once a guest has placed an order, make them feel good about it. Tell them the strip flank steak looked excellent tonight or that the salmon just came in today. Don't tell them that the pork is a better choice than the steak! Encourage your guests' food choices. The simple act, on your part, of telling them that you've tasted what they're ordering and it's great can take away any anxiety they have about making a bad choice.

Make personal recommendations

Tell your guests what you like. It's always nice to be sincere about your food. Your enthusiasm will be infectious, even if guests don't order what you recommend. It won't bother them that you're excited about what's on the menu.

Bring extra napkins

If the guests order a meal that is particularly messy, such as barbecued ribs or lobster in butter sauce, bring them extra napkins before they ask. You should also bring extra napkins when customers dine with children.

Anticipate needs

Bringing a customer something before they ask is an excellent way to win the customer over. If you know a particular brand of Scotch is very strong, for example, bring the guest a glass of water with the drink they requested. If you are serving red beans and rice, drop off the Tabasco sauce at the same time.

Always feel free to ask your guests beforehand so they don't think you're imposing specific items on them. For example, if a guest orders the red beans and rice, you can say something like, "You would like to me to bring Tabasco sauce with that?"

Fast Fact

Eight out of 10 consumers say that dining out with friends and family is a better use of their time than cooking meals at home and cleaning up.[26]

Coffee refills

Make sure you provide coffee refills, but also be sure they ask before you pour. The guest might find it annoying to have the cup refilled without being asked. If a half-filled cup has been sitting for a while, replace the cup with a fresh one rather than filling the lukewarm cup.

"Doggie" bags

Take an extra moment with the "doggie" bags. Rather than dropping a box off with the customer to fill, fill containers in the kitchen. Also make sure you have appropriately sized and shaped containers for leftovers. When the customer arrives home and finds her flourless chocolate torte sideways in a soup container, it will not reflect well on you — or the restaurant.

Keep an eye on your tables

Even if you're waiting on another table, you should keep an eye on your other tables. If you see a guest looking around, stop over immediately and ask if there is anything you can get them.

Mindful of the disabled

If someone comes in for dinner who is blind, ask the guest if you can offer their seeing-eye dog some water or something to eat. You should also be particularly mindful of guests in wheelchairs. Make sure you sit them somewhere comfortable out of walkways.

Older guests

Another way to give value-added service is to make special arrangements for older guests. Be sure you are knowledgeable about the menu's nutritional content. Respond to elderly customers with patience and respect. They will certainly appreciate it and will tip accordingly.

Adding festivity

Is someone at the table celebrating a birthday? Try to make the evening festive for the customers. Some restaurants have special desserts for birthdays and other occasions. Other establishments have the entire staff sing to the individual. Even a simple balloon at a table makes the evening seem a bit more festive.

Tell the cooks good news

Just like you need to be sensitive to the mood of your guests, be sensitive to the mood of the kitchen crew. The cooks don't want to hear about things just when they're wrong; pass along good news to them and they will probably make it easier for you to take great care of your guests.

Make your movements invisible

That means move with the speed of the room. Good service is invisible: food and drinks simply arrive without a thought on the customer's part.

If the room is quiet, don't buzz around in it. If it's more upbeat, move a little quicker. You'll find fitting in seamlessly with the atmosphere will increase your guest's enjoyment — and it's a great way to stay focused.

Talk it up

Tell guests about specific events at your restaurant and invite them to return. It provides an opportunity to build personal connections. For example, invite guests to return for your rib special on Tuesdays. It's far more effective than just saying, "Thanks. Come again." While you're at it, invite them to sit in your section. You'll be more likely to remember their names and what they like. Some of the best tippers will be your regulars.

23. Statista, 2016.
24. Reserve, 2016.
25. National Restaurant Association, 2016.
26. Reserve, 2016.

Chapter 7

Dealing with the Dark Side

Not every aspect of serving is full of great tippers and happy campers — there is definitely a dark side. This chapter will cover how to deal with complaining customers, difficult customers, drunk costumers — you name it.

Servers who forecasted great weather increased their tips by almost 4 percent. Say something like, "The weather is supposed to be great today! Enjoy it!"[27]

Fast Fact

Handling Customer Complaints

One of the most difficult duties is to receive complaints from customers and make satisfactory adjustments. Customer complaints are an opportunity to turn the situation around and make a lifelong customer. Complaints that aren't handled the right way can make the customer disgruntled.

In handling complaints, you should:

1. Approach the customer with a friendly spirit.
2. Listen to the complaint, and try to get the whole story.
3. Restate the gist of the complaint and have the customer confirm this summarized statement.
4. Express sincere regret for the occurrence.
5. Offer to exchange or substitute food that is unsatisfactory.
6. Refer to the restaurant's policies when relevant.
7. When the refusal of a request is necessary, explain the reason clearly.
8. When the restaurant is at fault, apologize and promise that an effort will be made to prevent the situation in the future.
9. Thank the customer for making the complaint, saying, "I am glad you told me," or "Thank you for bringing this to my attention."
10. When the customer makes a return visit, see that the service is faultless and that she has no further cause for complaint.
11. Refer difficult and unreasonable complaints to the manager.
12. Report all serious complaints and those involving business policy and regulations to management.

Dealing with Difficult Customers

Some customers are difficult to deal with because of their attitudes or special needs; they should be handled with intelligence and good judgment. Here are some examples:

*   **The early customer**. Receive him courteously and explain when service will begin. Offer him a comfortable seat and give him a newspaper or magazine.

- **The late customer**. Make her feel welcome. If the food selection is limited, explain that it's near closing time. Try to provide good service without making her feel that she is being hurried.

- **The hurried customer**. Recommend counter service if this is available. Tell him in advance approximately how long the service will take. Give the best service possible under the circumstances.

- **The over-familiar customer**. Be courteous but dignified with her; avoid long conversations; stay away from the table except when actual service is needed.

- **The grouchy customer**. Meet him cheerfully, and treat him pleasantly. Don't argue with him. Listen to his complaints courteously, but don't encourage him. Do not be distressed by unreasonable complaints.

- **The angry customer**. Listen to her, express regret at the occurrence that prompted her complaint, thank her for calling it to your attention, and try to resolve the problem.

- **The troublemaker**. Be courteous, but don't be drawn into arguments. Do not participate in criticisms of the management or make statements that may be taken as complaints about the restaurant.

- **The tired customer**. Seat her at a quiet table. In cold weather, suggest a hot soup, a hot drink, and some particularly appetizing light food. On a hot day, suggest a chilled salad or a frosted drink.

Handling Problems

Unfortunately, on occasion, things don't go well and a customer has a problem or becomes a problem. The following are a few common problems that might arise and ways to deal with them.

The drunk customer

Excessive alcohol consumption must be controlled in the dinning room for the sake of other customers and for the liability to the restaurant and yourself. When a customer has had too much to drink, it's often hard to reason with him or her, and the customer can become angry or argumentative very quickly. Don't do anything that would suggest you are being confrontational.

- Try to get the customer to see that you're on his side. Tell the guest that you are concerned for his ability to drive home and you want to see him remain safe.

- Try to get the guest to eat something. It's a good way to metabolize the alcohol already in the guest's system. If the guest refuses to order, try getting him or her something on the house.

- If a guest refuses to eat and leaves drunk, the restaurant is legally required to notify the police. Let the guest know this, and try to get him or her to come back, sit down, and eat something.

- If the guest is with a companion, it might make more sense to try to reason with that guest rather than the intoxicated one.

- Be sure to file a report with your manager concerning the incident.

- If you are uncomfortable dealing with an intoxicated guest or the situation escalates, be sure to get your manger involved.

The rowdy table

Rowdy tables can be very disruptive to your other customers. The accept-able noise level is partially determined by the type of establishment — people will be much louder in a sports bar than a fine-dining restaurant. If you have a table that is getting out of control, you must make them aware of the situation. Notify your manager, and they will talk with the head of the party and ask them to quiet down. If the guest refuses to cooperate, they will have to be asked to leave.

Half of all adults have had held a restaurant job at some point in their lives.[28]

Pets

The only pet most departments of health will allow in a restaurant are seeing-eye dogs. If a restaurant has an outdoor seating area, however, they will often allow pets there. If someone tries to bring in a pet that is not an assistive animal, tell them that the restaurant does not allow animals, and show the owner to an outside table where the pet can stay while the owner dines. Some restaurants also provide bowls of water and have biscuits on hand for these situations — this can go a long way in keeping your customer, who is also a pet owner, happy!

The well-known guest

Famous people and other well-known personalities often want to dine in peace and not be disturbed by someone wanting an autograph or someone wanting to start a conversation. You should find the guest an out-of-the-way table and serve the guest just like any other customer.

Accidents

Accidents, large and small, are bound to happen on your shift. If a small accident happens, such as a spill, it can be easily and quickly dealt with. If you or a customer spills something on the table, quickly move all items to the other side, place a clean napkin on the spill, then return all the items to their original positions. If something is spilled on the customer, you should help the guest clean up the spill and apologize.

If a more serious accident happens, immediately notify your manager. Your manager can determine whether medical care is necessary. Whatever the accident is, the first thing you should do is attend to the guest. Afterward, be sure to follow any policy your restaurant has about logging or recording accidents with an accident report. Be sure you include the name of the guest, your name, the date and time, and a complete description of the incident.

CASE STUDY: Brittany Morstatter

Bartender
Over 13 years in and out of the restaurant industry, beginning at age 17

Although the phrase "the customer is always right" is one of the most ridiculous things I've ever heard ¬— you'll encounter MANY situations of that being false — it's still a good general rule to follow. You're entering into the "hospitality" industry; your title is literally "server."

Be attentive to your guests' needs, and learn to anticipate them! A family with kids comes in, so ensure they have extra napkins. A group of guys come to try your restaurant's "heat" challenge, so load them up with plenty of water (and be prepared to watch the tears stream and laugh alongside them). It's pretty easy to be a good waitress: smile, be friendly, and give your guests what they need. And believe me, they don't need your sass or attitude.

Worst restaurant experience: While serving one night in the Buffalo Wild Wings bar area (think high bar tables), I was hustling — it was a busy weekend night — and went to rush around the corner on my way to the kitchen and a little girl, under two years old, was running loose, and she bounced off my legs and flew back a few feet! I was mortified, but a few kisses from her grandma and she was perfectly fine. (The grandmother also apologized to me because the little one shouldn't have been running loose.) After that, I didn't sacrifice safety for quicker service.

Best restaurant experience: Generally, any time someone comes in and requests me or only comes in when I'm working. It's so rewarding and encouraging that I'm doing a great job when someone prefers my service.

Starting as a hostess at a local, small-town restaurant, Brittany quickly moved to server and held various serving and bartending jobs since, both in national chain restaurants and small-town establishments, including a tavern and a golf course clubhouse. After graduating college, Brittany spent over four years with Buffalo Wild Wings in various positions: bartender, server, certified trainer, FOH manager, and certified trainer manager.

27. Shin, 2014.
28. Reserve, 2016.

Chapter 8

Understanding Alcohol

If you work for a restaurant that has a wine and beer or liquor license, alcohol sales can be a huge source of revenue and, therefore, tips. Unfortunately, it can also be a liability. In recent years, the newspapers have been full of stories about restaurants and/or employees being sued because a patron was driving in a drunken state and hurt or killed someone on the way home. The first step in responsible alcohol sales is to be sure that you know the laws and ramifications of the laws that affect alcohol sales.

Know the signs of intoxication. These can include slurred speech, loss of inhibition, aggressiveness, and loss of muscle coordination.

Know your restaurant's alcohol sales policy. This policy should include a description of federal, state, and local laws that govern your alcohol sales. It should also lay down a set of rules for your servers, including not selling to minors and intoxicated customers. You should also set limits. For example, put a policy into place that says if a customer has four drinks, the server should notify the manager. The manager can then monitor the situation and determine whether or not the customer needs to be cut off. You may also want to set up a relationship with a local cab company for those occasions when you need to suggest a cab to one of your patrons.

If an incident happens. Make sure you get management involved immediately. Also, document everything that happens.

Resources. The National Restaurant Association Educational Foundation offers training materials related to responsible beverage-alcohol service. You can find this information at: **www.nraef.org**. The website **www.restaurantbeast.com** offers free downloads of an alcohol awareness brochure, an alcohol awareness test for servers, a blood alcohol concentration (BAC) guide, and a state BAC reference. You can also find information about alcohol abuse at **www.icap.org**, the International Center for Alcohol Policies' website.

Alcohol Safety

Facts

Blood Alcohol Concentration (BAC) is an indicator of how much alcohol is in the bloodstream. Alcohol is absorbed directly into the bloodstream from the stomach and intestines.

At 0-10 a person is considered legally intoxicated in most states. In our state the level of legal intoxication is_____.

Factors that affect the absorption of alcohol into the bloodstream include:

- Amount consumed
- How quickly the alcohol is consumed
- A person's weight

- A person's gender
- Whether or not a person has eaten recently

Ways to help prevent a guest from becoming intoxicated:

- Always check IDs
- Do not serve the guest more than one drink at a time
- Offer guest food when drinking
- Keep track of how much a guest is consuming

Know the stages of intoxication:

Level 1

- Guest gets louder
- Guest may become overly friendly

Level 2

- Guest may have difficulty walking
- Speech may be slurred
- Guest may become argumentative
- Guest may have reduced muscle coordination (may have trouble picking up change, etc.)

How to Serve Alcohol

While you don't need to understand the distilling or fermenting processes, you should be familiar with different types of alcohol, different glasses, and the basic terminology:

Serving – Waitstaff should always serve alcoholic beverages promptly. How quickly someone gets their drink can set the tone and mood for the entire evening. If you don't get there with the drink for 10 minutes, the customer realizes his or her meal service will probably be just as slow. If you're really busy, a host or manager should step in and see that the table receives the drinks quickly. As with food, women are generally served first.

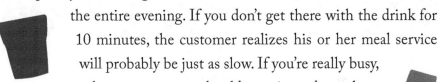

Types of glasses – Different glasses are used for different drinks. Make sure you know the difference between a jigger, highball glass, martini glass, and champagne flute, as well as the difference between red and white wine glasses. Make sure you always pick up glassware correctly. You should never touch the rim; glasses should be picked up by the handle or the base in the case of a wine glass.

Types of alcohol – In addition to knowing glassware, you should be familiar with the different types of alcohol. For example, make sure you knows that the blanket term "whiskey" can refer to Irish whiskey, bourbon, rye, scotch, blended, and Canadian.

Types of Alcohol

All liquor served in the restaurant can be divided into two basic categories: *well* items and *call* items. Some restaurants establish a three-tier system: well, call, and premium liquor. Premium liqour would cost the most.

Whiskey

All whiskeys are distilled from fermented grains. Commonly used grains are barley, rye, corn, and wheat. All whiskeys are aged in oak barrels. From this aging process, they obtain their characteristic color, flavor, and aroma.

You can spell it whiskey or whisky — both spellings are technically correct. The Scots leave out the "e" while the Irish leave it in.[29]

Most whiskey consumed in this country is produced in either the United States, Canada, Scotland, or Ireland. Each country produces its very own distinctive whiskeys. Whiskey can be divided into two basic types: **straight whiskey** and **blended whiskey**.

Straight whiskey is a whiskey that has never been mixed with other types of whiskey or with any neutral grain spirits. Straight whiskey itself has four major types, which will be discussed below.

Blended whiskey is a blend of straight whiskeys and/or neutral grain spirits. It must contain at least 20 percent, by volume, of a straight whiskey and should be bottled at no less than 80 proof.

Straight Whiskey

Bourbon whiskey: Its name is derived from Bourbon county in Kentucky, where the whiskey was originally produced. Bourbon must be distilled from grain mash containing at least 51 percent corn.

Rye whiskey: Rye has the similar amber color of bourbon, but the flavor and aroma are different. Rye whiskey must be distilled from a fermented mash of grain containing at least 51 percent rye.

Corn whiskey: Corn whiskey must be distilled from fermented mash of grain containing at least 80 percent corn.

Bottled in bond whiskey: Usually a rye or bourbon whiskey that is produced under the supervision of the U.S. government. The government ensures the following:

- The whiskey is aged at least four years.
- It is bottled at 100 proof.
- It is produced in one distilling by a single distiller.
- It is bottled and stored under government supervision.

Since the government bonds these steps, the whiskey is referred to as "bottled in bond." The government doesn't guarantee the quality of the whiskey; it only ensures that these steps have been completed under its supervision.

Blended Whiskey

Canadian whiskey: Canadian whiskey is a blend produced under the supervision of the Canadian government. This whiskey is usually lighter-bodied than most American whiskeys.

Scotch whiskey: Scotch whiskey is produced only in Scotland. All Scotch blends contain malt and grain whiskeys. The unique smoky flavor of Scotch is derived from drying malted barley over open peat fires.

Irish whiskey: Irish whiskey is produced only in Ireland. This whiskey is usually heavier and fuller bodied than most Scotch blends. The malted barley used in the distilling process is dried over coal-fired kilns. This drying process has little or no affect on the whiskey's taste.

Fast Fact

The most expensive whiskey ever sold was a bottle of Macallan "M" in a large crystal decanter. It sold in Hong Kong for over $600,000.[30]

Vodka

Vodka was originally produced in Russia from distilled potatoes. Now produced in various countries, vodka is commonly made from a variety of grains, the most common of which are wheat and corn. It is bottled at no less than 80 and no higher than

110 proof. During the distillation process, it is highly refined and filtered, usually through activated charcoal. Vodka is not aged. It is colorless, odorless, and virtually tasteless. Because of these traits, it is a very versatile liquor that can be mixed with almost anything.

Gin

Gin is distilled from a variety of grains and is bottled at 80 proof. Every gin manufactured has its own distinctive flavor and aroma. The aroma is derived from a recipe of juniper berries and other assorted plants. Gin is usually colorless and is most often  used in making martinis. Vacuum-distilled gin is distilled in a glass-lined vacuum at lower than normal distilling temperature. This process tends to eliminate the bitterness found in some gins.

Rum

Rum is distilled from cane syrup, which is the fermented juice of sugar cane and molasses. It is bottled at no less than 80 proof. Most rums are a blend of many different types of aged rums. Dark rums often have caramel syrup added for color.

Rums can be classified into two major types:

1. **Light-bodied rums** are dry and light in color due to a lack of molasses. Among the light-bodied rums are two varieties: gold label and white label. The gold is often of slightly better quality and is darker and sweeter; the white is paler and slightly stronger in flavor.

2. **Heavy-bodied rums** have been distilled by a different and slower process. Because of the slowness of this process, the rum contains more molasses, which makes the rum darker, sweeter, and richer.

Brandy

Brandy is traditionally distilled from a mash of fermented grapes but may
be produced from other
fruits. There are many different types available.

Cognac is perhaps the finest of distilled brandies. It is produced only in the Cognac region of France. Usually, it is a blend of many different types of distilled cognac of the region. Cognac may be aged for as long as 50 years or more.

Did You Know?

The four most common ways to label cognac, from least expensive to most expensive, are "VS, VSOP, XO, and Extra." These are mainly ranked by age, price, and quality. With the cheap stuff, no one will really care if you ask for a mixer, but when you get to the XO or Extra — usually hundreds or thousands of dollars per bottle — you'll start getting weird looks unless you ask for it neat. [31]

Armagnac brandy is similar to cognac but slightly drier in taste. It is produced only in the Armagnac region of France.

Apple Jack is distilled from the cider of crushed apples. Calvados (an apple brandy) is produced only in Normandy, France. In the United States, Apple Jack is often bottled in bond.

Fruit flavored brandies have a distilled brandy base with a flavor ingredient added. These are commonly used in blended cocktails.

Tequila

Tequila is usually produced in Mexico or the American south-west. It is distilled from the fermented mash of the aqua or century plants, which are cacti. Tequila is usually clear, although some types may have a gold tint.

The smell and taste are distinctive. Tequila is used primarily in making margaritas. Also, in recent years, there has been a wide increase in the variety of "premium" tequilas. Tequila can also be chilled and served as a shot.

Fast Fact

If someone orders a shot of tequila with "training wheels," it means they want salt and lime with it.

Cordials and Liqueurs

Cordials and liqueurs are created by the mixing or pre-distilling of neutral grain spirits with fruits, flowers, or plants to which sweeteners have been added. Cordials and liqueurs are all colorful and very sweet in taste, which is why they are usually served as after-dinner drinks. There are a wide variety of cordials and liqueurs available.

Beer

There are five basic categories for the hundreds of brands of beer produced. They are:

1. **Lagers:** the most popular type produced today

2. **Ales:** these contain more hops and are stronger in flavor

3. **Porters:** dark and bitter

4. **Stouts:** dark and strong

5. **Bocks:** dark and strong; brewed in the fall and drunk in the spring

---

Did You Know?

There isn't a huge difference between porters and stouts. However, porters generally use malted barley while stouts generally use unmalted roasted barley. This is why many people associate stouts with a coffee flavor. [32]

Beer is available in bottles, cans, or on draft. Of the hundreds of brands available, fewer than a dozen are primarily demanded by customers. However, it should be noted that the popularity of "micro-brewed" beers has increased a ton over the past couple of years. There are many independent and chain restaurants that use a micro-brewery in their own establishment as a marketing vehicle.

Imported beers have gained increasing popularity in recent years. Although they are 50 to 100 percent more expensive than domestic beers, customers still want them.

Light beer is produced with fewer calories than other beer, and has developed a great demand within the past five years. One to two light beers should be included on your list.

Top 5 Most Popular Imported Beers in America[33]

1. Corona Extra
2. Heineken
3. Modelo Especial
4. Corona Light
5. Stella Artois

Bar Terms

Here are some common bar terms:

Alcohol: There are several types of alcohol. Ethyl alcohol is the type found in all alcoholic beverages.

Proof: Proof is the measurement of alcohol in an alcoholic beverage. Each degree of proof represents a half percent of alcohol. For example, a bottle of liquor distilled at 90 proof is 45 percent alcohol.

Grain-neutral spirits: This is a colorless, tasteless, usually odorless ethyl alcohol distilled from grain at a minimum of 190 proof. Grain-neutral spirits are used in blending whiskies and in making other types of liquor/liqueur.

Muddle – This is when you grind up ingredients with a special tool called a muddler. You do this when you want to draw out specific flavors from ingredients. This is done with mint in Mojitos as well as oranges and cherries in Old Fashioneds.

Neat: This means no ice. Guests will often order whiskey "neat," which just means a short glass with a shot of whiskey in it at room temperature.

Shot or jigger: A shot or jigger is a unit of liquor ranging from ¾ ounce to 2 ounces. Most restaurants pour 1 ¼–1 ½-ounce shots for cocktails, and add slightly less to blended drinks.

Straight up: This refers to a cocktail that is served with no ice — usually a martini, Manhattan or margarita. A special chilled, long-stem, straight-up glass should be used. Liqueurs and cordials that are served straight up may be poured into pony glasses.

On the rocks: This refers to a cocktail — usually a straight liquor, such as a scotch or a cordial — being served over ice. Although most cocktails are served over ice anyway, certain cocktails and liquors are just as commonly served without ice. In such cases the bartender or cocktail waitress must ask the customer which way she prefers.

Twist, wedge and **slice:** refer to the fruit that garnishes the cocktail glass. A twist is a lemon peel. A wedge or slice is usually a piece of lime or orange.

Press: Use a fruit press to squeeze the juice of a fruit garnish into the cocktail.

Bitters: is a commercially produced liquid made from roots, berries or a variety of herbs. It is, indeed, bitter, and a dash or two is used in some cocktails.

Virgin: refers to a drink that contains no alcohol, such as a Virgin Piña-Colada or a Virgin Bloody Mary.

Back: Usually refers to either a water or coffee back. This indicates that along with the cocktail ordered, the customer would also like a separate glass of water or cup of coffee. (Ex: "I'll take a beer back with my shot.")

Rimmed: Place either salt, sugar, or celery salt around the rim of a cocktail glass. Usually Bloody Marys, Margaritas, and Salty Dogs are served this way. The bartender prepares a rimmed glass by wetting the rim of the glass with a wedge of fruit; he then twirls the glass in a bowl of the salt or sugar desired.

Shaken: refers to a cocktail that is shaken in the mixing glass before being strained.

Stirred: refers to a cocktail that is stirred (not shaken) in the mixing glass with a spoon before being strained.

Wine

Serving wine can be as simplistic or as elaborate as you want. Some restaurants stock hundreds of bottles, many of rare vintages and kept in elaborate cellars. Others serve only a few house wines. Wine, regardless of the quality or cost, will always improve the customer's evening by enhancing the flavor of the entrées and making dinner a festive event.

It's important that you know the basics about wine, the most common grape varieties, and how people discuss wine. If you work in a restaurant that specializes in or carries wine, you should be able to discuss wines' color and smell ("nose") and taste ("palate"). You may also want to be able to distinguish more subtle color differences. Is the wine yellow like a Chardonnay, or is it clearer like a Pinot Grigio?

Some of the terms people use to describe smell and taste include dry, sweet, earthy, and smoky. They may also say that a wine's taste is reminiscent of another flavor, such as raspberries or pepper. Most importantly, your servers should know which wines in your establishment are sweet and which are dry. This will be the main category upon which guests will base their wine decisions.

You need to be familiar with the restaurant's wine list and how all the wines taste. If the customer is particularly wine savvy, you could suggest getting a manager or someone else with greater wine knowledge to help. You should also let customers have a taste of the wines that you offer by the glass — just check with management that a small sample is acceptable.

Serving wine

Red wines should be served at room temperature, and white wines should be chilled to about 50 degrees. To serve a bottle of wine, present the bottle to the person that ordered it, with the label facing the customer. Once the customer has approved the wine, set the bottle on the corner of the table to open it.

Cut the foil off the lower lip of the bottle top and put the foil in your apron pocket. Remove the cork and pour an ounce or two for the person who ordered it to taste. You can also set the cork beside this person so they can inspect it, if they choose. After the customer has tasted and approved the wine, pour the wine for all the guests partaking, starting with the women in the group.

When you finish pouring a glass, give the bottle a half turn as you raise it to help keep from making spills. Also keep a napkin next to the bottleneck to catch any spills. When filling wine glasses, fill to one-half or two-thirds.

Opening sparkling wine and champagne:

1. Always use a napkin behind the bottle to stop drips, and although it rarely happens, it is possible that the bottle may split from the internal pressure.

2. Remove the foil and wire muzzle.

3. Remove the cork by turning the bottle, not the cork. Always point the bottle away from people. The cork should be removed slowly and carefully, it should never explode open with a gush of champagne.

4. Special champagne glasses may be used, however it is perfectly acceptable to serve champagne in tulip-shaped wine glasses.

5. A stuck cork may be removed by placing the neck of the bottle under a stream of hot water for a few seconds. The heat will build up pressure on the inside of the bottle making it easier to extract the cork.

Tasting tips

Seeing – You can tell several things from the color of a wine, including its age; white wines grow darker with age, and red wines grow lighter.

Swirling – Smell is an important part of wine tasting. In order to smell all the nuances in a wine, you want to swirl the wine in your glass to "open it up." Swirling allows air to combine with the wine. To swirl, hold the glass by its stem and rotate in a small circle.

Smelling – After swirling the wine, smell it and try to describe the aroma.

Sipping – When tasting wine, you should take small amounts into your mouth and hold them at the bottom of your mouth. Draw in air through a small hole in your lips and let the air cross the wine in your mouth, allowing it to bubble.

Here are some ways to describe wine:

- **Light** – Refers to the wine's body and/or alcohol content.

- **Dry** – Refers to the lack of sweetness in the wine.

- **Semi-Sweet** – Refers to the underlying sweetness of a wine.

- **Body** – The texture or taste of the wine in the mouth.

- **Bouquet** – Many aromas are found in a single wine.

- **Buttery** – Rich, creamy aroma and flavor. Usually used to describe some Chardonnays.

- **Finish** – The flavor a wine leaves in the mouth after the wine is swallowed.

- **Legs** – The drops of wine that run down the inside of the glass when it is swirled.

- **Mature** – Ready to drink.

- **Nose** – The aroma or bouquet of a wine.

- **Bright** – A young wine with fresh, fruity flavors.

- **Chewy** – Heavy, tannic, full-bodied wines.

- **Crisp** – A noticeably acidic wine, but the acid does not overpower the wine.

- **Dense** – A full-flavored wine or wine with a deep color.

- **Earthy** – Can be a positive or negative characteristic. It may refer to a pleasant, clean quality or a funky, dirty character.

- **Fat** – A full-bodied, high-alcohol wine.

- **Forward** – An early maturing wine.

- **Fragrant** – A wine with a floral aroma or bouquet.

- **Jammy** – A sweet, concentrated fruit flavor.

- **Peppery** – A wine with a spicy, black pepper flavor.

- **Robust** – Full-flavored, intense wine.

- **Round** – A wine with a well-balanced, mellow and full-bodied flavor.

- **Soft** – A wine that is mellow and well balanced.

- **Aggressive** – The wine has slightly high tannins or acid.

- **Flat** – A wine that lacks flavor due to the lack of acidity in it.

- **Metallic** – A wine with a tin-like flavor.

- **Off** – A wine that is flawed or spoiled.

- **Sharp** – A wine with too much acid.

The more you know about the drinks you serve, the more impressed your guests will be with your service. And impressive service equals better tips.

---

29. Whisky for Everyone, 2011.
30. Lord, 2014.
31. Porges, 2013.
32. Teeter, 2015.
33. Malin, 2015.

Chapter 9

Restaurant Safety

Workplace accidents happen. How you respond to them can be the difference between life and death. The first thing to do is to have a safety plan in place.

Preventing Accidents

Accidents are both dangerous and costly. Most accidents are avoidable and are the results of people being careless such as:

- Failure to immediately clean up foods spilled on the floor to prevent anyone slipping

- Failure to set trays and dishes back from the edges of the side tables or counters so that they will not be knocked off in passing

- Loading trays in such a way that the dishes will slide off

- Piling dishes in tall stacks that may tip easily

- Failure to nest cups by turning the handles in opposite directions to make them fit together securely

- Stacking piles of dishes unevenly so that the stack is likely to tip

- Carrying several water glasses in the fingers so that the rims touch (they frequently are cracked or nicked by this method of handling)

- Failure to keep long handles on containers turned away from the edges of the hot plates or counters

- Leaving cupboard doors ajar so that a person may hit the corner and be injured

- Failure to enter the serving pantry and kitchen by the entrance door ("In") and to leave by the exit door ("Out")

- Not watching the movement of other employees in the vicinity, and moving immediately into their paths without warning them

- Not warning the guests when plates, containers, or handles are very hot

- Failure to hold hot plates and handles with the side towel to avoid burns

Strains

Carrying equipment or food items that are too heavy can result in strains to the arms, legs, or back.

To prevent strains:

- Store heavy items on lower shelves
- Use dollies or carts when moving objects that are too heavy to carry
- Use carts with firm shelves and properly operating wheels or casters to move objects from one area to another
- Don't carry too many objects at one time; instead, use a cart
- Don't try to lift large or heavy objects by yourself
- Use proper lifting techniques; remember to bend from your knees, not your back

Slipping and Falling

Anyone who slips and falls can be badly hurt. To prevent slips and falls:

- Clean up wet spots and spills immediately.

- Let people know when floors are wet. Use signs that signal caution, and prominently display them. Wear non-slip shoes.

- Do not stack boxes or other objects too high; they can fall and cause people to trip.

- Keep items such as boxes, ladders, step stools, and carts out of the paths of foot traffic.

There are approximately 624,301 restaurants in the United States.[34]

Choking

As kids, we probably all heard our parents say: "Don't eat so fast! Chew your food properly!" They may have added, "Don't talk while you're eating," and "Drink your milk carefully!" It's good advice for children — and for adults. Anyone can choke on food if they're not careful. That's why an important part of food service safety is being alert to your customers.

Over 4,000 people die annually from accidental choking in the United States.

Here's what to look for and what to do:

- If a person has both hands to the throat and cannot speak or cough, he or she is probably choking.

- If this person can talk, cough, or breathe, don't pat him or her on the back or interfere in any way.

- If this person can't talk, cough, or breathe, you'll need to take action. Use the Heimlich Maneuver, and call for help immediately.

Heimlich Maneuver

Avoid Bacterial Cross-Contamination

One of the most common causes of food-borne illness is cross-contamination: the transfer of bacteria from food to food, hand to food, or equipment to food. While most cross-contamination cases occur in the back-of-the-house, servers can cause this situation, as well. An example of this is using the same cutting board to cut salad tomatoes and to slice raw chicken. Keep separate cutting boards for the salad and server areas.

Food to food: Raw, contaminated ingredients may be added to foods, or fluids from raw foods may drip into foods that receive no further cooking. A common mistake is to leave thawing meat on a top shelf in the refrigerator where it can drip down onto prepared foods stored below.

Hand to food: Bacteria are found throughout the body: in the hair, on the skin, in clothing, in the mouth, nose and throat, in the intestinal tract, and on scabs or scars from skin wounds. These bacteria often end up on the hands where they can easily spread to food. People can also pick up bacteria by touching raw food, then transfer it to cooked or ready-to-eat food.

Equipment to food: Bacteria may pass from equipment to food when equipment that has touched contaminated food is then used to prepare other food without proper cleaning and sanitizing. For example, cross-contamination can occur when surfaces used for cutting raw poultry are then used to cut foods that will be eaten raw, such as fresh vegetables.

Coverings, such as plastic wrap and holding and serving containers, can also harbor bacteria that can spread to food. A can opener, a plastic-wrap box, or a food slicer can also become a source of cross-contamination if not properly sanitized between uses.

Unsanitary practices. Unsanitary practices you should avoid include chewing gum, eating food in food-preparation areas, and tasting food using your fingers. Also, make sure you cover any cuts, and use gloves when handling food.

Danger zone. Keep foods out of the temperature danger zone (45° to 140°F). Make sure to keep hot foods hot and cod foods cold.

Thawing foods. Thaw foods in the refrigerator, microwave, or under cold, running water. If using the running water method, do not leave foods out for more than two hours, and cook immediately upon thawing.

Reheating food. Do not use a steam table to reheat foods. Also, be sure that when reheating, you bring the food's temperature up to 165°F.

Cooling food. When cooling soups or stews, put it in several shallow pans so it will cool quickly. You can also use an ice bath to expedite the cooling process.

FIFO. Be sure to stress importance of "first in, first out" method of storage. This will ensure foods don't become outdated. Also be sure to label, date and cover all food items, and keep cleaning supplies in a separate storage area.

Dinner is the most popular meal in casual dining restaurants.[35]

Fast Fact

Bacteria Primer

Bacteria are everywhere: in the air, in all areas of the restaurant, and all over one's body. Most bacteria are microscopic and of no harm to people. Many forms of bacteria are actually beneficial, aiding in the production of such things as cheese, bread, butter, alcoholic beverages, etc. Only a small percentage of bacteria will cause food to spoil and can generate a form of food poisoning when consumed.

Bacteria need food, water, and warmth in order to survive. Their growth rate depends upon how favorable these conditions are. Bacteria prefer to ingest moisture-saturated foods, such as meats, dairy products, and produce. They will not grow as readily on dry foods such as cereals, sugar, or flour.

Bacteria will grow most rapidly when the temperature is between 85°– 100°F. In most cases, the growth rate will slow down drastically if the temperature is hotter or colder than this. Thus, it is vitally important that perishable food items are refrigerated before bacteria have a chance to establish themselves and multiply. Certain bacteria can survive in extreme hot- and cold-temperature ranges. By placing these bacteria in severe temperatures you will be slowing down their growth rate, but not necessarily killing them.

The greatest problem in controlling bacteria is their rapid reproduction cycle. Approximately every 15 minutes the bacteria count will double under optimal living conditions. The more bacteria present, the greater the chance of bacterial infection. This is why food products that must be subjected to conditions favorable to bacteria are done so for the shortest period possible.

An important consideration when handling food products is that bacteria need several hours to adjust to a new environment before they are able to begin rapidly multiplying. Thus, if you had removed a food product from the walk-in refrigerator and had inadvertently introduced bacteria to it, advanced growth would not begin for several hours. If you had immediately placed the item back into the walk-in, the temperature would have killed the bacteria before it became established.

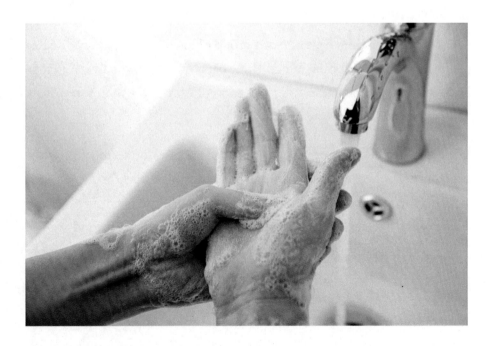

Bacterial forms do not have a means of transportation; they must be introduced to an area by some other vehicle. People are primarily responsible for transporting bacteria to new areas. The body temperature of 98.6°F is perfect for bacterial existence and proliferation. A person coughing, sneezing or wiping their hands on a counter can introduce bacteria to an area. Bacteria may be transmitted also by insects, air, water and articles onto which they have attached themselves, such as boxes, blades, knives and cutting boards.

Dangerous forms of bacteria

The following section describes a number of harmful bacteria that may be found in a restaurant. The technical names and jargon are given for your own information. The important points to retain are the causes and preventive actions for each.

Clostridium Perfringens

Clostridium perfringens is one of a group of bacterial infectious diseases that will cause a poisoning effect. These bacteria are extremely dangerous because they are tasteless, odorless and colorless, and therefore nearly impossible to detect.

Clostridium perfringens are usually found in meat or seafood that was previously cooked and then held at room temperature for a period of time. These perfringens are anaerobic. They do not need air in order to survive. They can thrive in masses of food or in canned foods in the form of botulism. In order to survive, the bacterium will form a spore and surround itself. The spore will protect the bacterium from exposure to the air and give it a much wider temperature range for survival than normal bacteria: 65°–120°F. These bacterial forms may survive through long periods of extreme temperature and then multiply when the conditions are more favorable.

Keeping cooked food consistently above 148°F or below 40°F eliminates clostridium perfringens bacteria.

Clostridium Botulism

This is another of the poisoning forms of bacteria. Botulism is a rare infectious disease but it is far more lethal than the other types. Botulism exists only in an air-free environment like that of canned goods. These bacteria are most often found in home-canned goods; however, several national food packers have reported outbreaks in their operations.

Symptoms such as vomiting, double vision, abdominal pain and shock may occur anytime from three to four hours after ingestion to eight days later.

Examine all canned goods closely before using. Look for dented, leaking cans and swollen cans or jar tops.

Staphylococci Poisoning

Staphylococci bacteria (Staph) are perhaps the most common cause of food poisoning. Staph bacteria can be found everywhere, particularly in the human nose. The bacteria by themselves are harmless. The problem arises when they are left uncontrolled to grow in food items. Food that has been left out, unrefrigerated, for just a few hours can produce the poisonous toxins of Staph bacteria.

Symptoms will appear two to six hours after consumption. Common symptoms are vomiting, muscle weakness, cramps and diarrhea. The sickness ranges from very severe cases — sometimes lethal — to a relatively mild illness. To prevent Staph poisoning, follow refrigeration procedures precisely. Only remove the refrigerated food items that you will be using right away.

Salmonella Infection

Salmonella infection is directly caused by the bacteria themselves, after consumption by a human. In certain cases, death has resulted; however, usually Salmonella cause severe, but temporary, illness. Symptoms are vomiting, fever, abdominal pain, and cramps. Symptoms usually show up 12–24 hours after consumption and may last for several days.

Salmonella are found in the intestinal tract of some animals. They have been discovered in some packaged foods, eggs, poultry, seafood and meat. Thorough cooking and following refrigeration procedures can keep Salmonella growth to a safe limit.

Hepatitis, dysentery, and diphtheria are some of the other infectious diseases that are bacterially derived.

Hygiene

Personal hygiene is the best way to stop bacteria from contaminating and spreading into new areas. Hands are the greatest source of contamination. Hands must be washed constantly throughout the day. Every time an individual scratches her head or sneezes, she is exposing her hands to bacteria and will spread it to anything she touches, such as food, equipment and clothes. Hand and nail brushes, antibacterial soaps, and disposable gloves should be a part of every restaurant, even if not required by law.

Every employee must practice good basic hygiene:

- Short hair and/or hair contained in a net
- Clean-shaven or facial hair contained in a net
- Clean clothes/uniforms
- Clean hands and short nails

- No unnecessary jewelry
- A daily shower or bath
- No smoking in or near the kitchen
- Hand-washing, prior to starting work, periodically, and after handling any foreign object: head, face, ears, money, food, boxes or trash

If you have the symptoms of the common cold or any open cuts or infections, you shouldn't go to work. By simply breathing, you might be inadvertently exposing the environment to bacteria.

American diners eat out more frequently during the summer.[36]

Hand-washing is perhaps the most critical aspect of good personal hygiene in food service.

Employees should wash their hands after the following activities:

- Smoking (hands come in contact with mouth)
- Eating (hands come in contact with mouth)
- Using the restroom
- Handling money
- Touching raw food (the raw food may contain bacteria)
- Touching or combing their hair
- Coughing, sneezing or blowing their nose
- Taking a break
- Handling anything dirty (touching a dirty apron or taking out the trash, for example)

Workers should wash their hands with soap and warm water for 20 seconds. When working with food, they should wash gloved hands as often as bare hands.

The proper hand-washing method is as follows:

1. Remove any jewelry.
2. Turn water on as hot as you can stand it.
3. Moisten hands and forearms up to elbows.
4. Lather them thoroughly with soap.
5. Wash for at least 20 seconds, rubbing hands together, washing between fingers and up to the elbows.
6. Use a brush for under nails.
7. Rinse hands and forearms with hot water.
8. Dry hands and forearms with a paper towel.

When handling tableware, you should:

- Use plastic gloves if directly handling gloves (remember, just because you have a glove on does not mean you can't cross-contaminate).
- Use plastic scoops in the ice machine.
- Avoid touching food contact surfaces. For instance, servers should not carry glasses by the rim and they should carry plates by the bottom or edge, keeping their hands away from eating surfaces. Employees should also pick up silverware by the handles.

The best impression is a clean impression. Make sure you're always being sanitary — if customers see you twirling your hair and then you deliver their food, they probably won't come back.

---

34. Statista, 2016.
35. Statista, 2016.
36. Statista, 2016.

Conclusion

orking in the res-
taurant industry
can be hard and
stressful work, but it can also be emotionally and
financially rewarding when your customers have
had a good experience.

Results from Zagat's "State of American Dining 2016" survey indicate just how important a
restaurant's waitstaff can be to customers. When
asked about bad dining experiences, the No. 1
complaint among participants was poor service
— easily beating noise, prices, and crowds.

The happiness of diners across the globe is in your hands! Take everything you've learned, and go earn yourself a spot in the "best server" hall of fame.

And make awesome money while doing it.

Appendix

FAQs About Tips

Because you're an employee, the tip income you receive, whether it's cash or included in a charge, is taxable income. As income, these tips are subject to federal income tax, Social Security and Medicare taxes, and possibly state income tax as well.

Q: *What tips do I have to report?*
A: If you received $20 or more in tips in any one month, you should report *all* your tips to your employer so that federal income tax, Social Security and Medicare taxes, and possibly state income tax can be withheld.

Q: *Do I have to report all my tips on my tax return?*
A: Yes. All tips are income and should be reported on your tax return.

Q: *Is it true that only 8 percent of my total sales must be reported as tips?*
A: No. You must report to your employer 100 percent of your tips, except for the tips *totaling* less than $20 in any month. The 8 percent rule only applies to employers.

Q: *Do I need to report tips from other employees?*
A: Yes. Employees who are indirectly tipped by other employees are required to report "tip-outs." This could apply to bus persons, for instance.

Q: *Do I have to report tip-outs that I pay to indirectly tipped employees?*
A: If you are a directly tipped employee, you should report to your employer only the amount of tips you retain. Maintain records of tip-outs with your other tip income (cash tips, charged tips, split tips, tip pool).

Q: *What records do I need to keep?*
A: You must keep a running daily log of all your tip income.

Q: *What can happen if I don't keep a record of my tips?*
A: Underreporting could result in your owing substantial taxes, penalties, and interest to the IRS and possibly other agencies.

Q: *If I report all my tips to my employer, do I still have to keep records?*
A: Yes. You should keep a daily log of your tips so that, in case of an examination, you can substantiate the actual amount of tips received.

Q: *Why should I report my tips to my employer?*
A: When you report your tip income to your employer, the employer is required to withhold federal income tax, Social Security and Medicare taxes, and possibly state income tax. Tip reporting may increase your Social Security credits, resulting in greater Social Security benefits when you retire. Tip reporting may also increase other benefits to which you may become entitled, such as unemployment benefits or retirement ben-

efits. Additionally, a greater income may improve financing approval for mortgages, car loans, and other loans.

Q: *I forgot to report my tip income to my employer, but I remembered to record it on my federal income tax return. Will that present a problem?*

A: If you do not report your tip income to your employer, but you do report the tip income on your federal income tax return, you may owe a 50 percent Social Security and Medicare tax penalty and be subject to a negligence penalty and, possibly, an estimated tax penalty.

Q: *If I report all my tips, but my taxes on the tips are greater than my pay from my employer, how do I pay the remaining taxes?*

A: You can either pay the tax when you file your federal income tax return or you can reach into your tip money and give some to your employer to be applied to those owed taxes.

Q: *What is my responsibility as an employee under the Tip Rate Determination Agreement (TRDA)?*

A: You are required to file your federal tax returns. You must sign a Tipped Employee Participation Agreement, proclaiming that you are participating in the program. To stay a participating employee, you must report tips at or above the tip rate determined by the agreement.

Q: *Who has to report tips?*

A: Employees who receive $20 or more in tips per month are required to report their tips in writing. For more information on employer tip reporting responsibilities, visit the IRS's website at **www.irs.gov**, and look at Publication 15, Circular E, Employer's Tax Guide. For more information on employee responsibilities, look at Publication 531, Reporting Tip Income.

Glossary

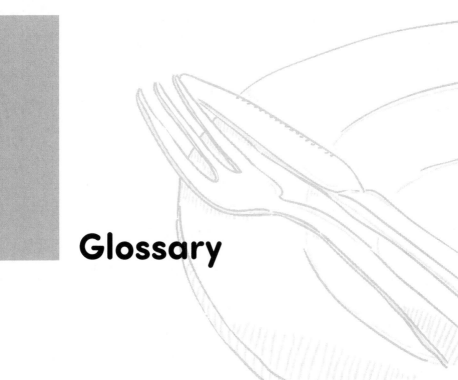

A la carte: Food items that are ordered and priced separately, unlike a set meal

Appetizer: A small portion of food or drink taken before a meal in order to stimulate the appetite

Arm service: When a server delivers meals by hand without aid of a tray or cart

Atmosphere: The sound, sight, smell, and overall feel of a location

Blood alcohol concentration: The concentration of alcohol in the bloodstream displayed as a percentage

Boning: The process of taking the bones out of meat or fish

Buffet: A meal with several dishes from which customers can pick and choose

Bussing: Clearing and cleaning a table after a customer's meal

Canapés: A tiny piece of pastry or bread with a topped with savory food

Clostridium Perfringens: A bacterium often found in the intestines of animals and on raw meat and poultry

CPR: Cardiopulmonary resuscitation, a life-saving emergency procedure that is performed when someone has stopped breathing or their heart has stopped

Critical control points: Specific food manufacturing procedures or steps where control can help reduce the possibility of food safety hazards

Cross-Contamination: When harmful bacteria or similar microorganisms are transferred from one object or substance to another

Daiquiri: A cocktail consisting of lime juice and rum

Entrée: A meal's main course

Expediter: A server whose main job is to increase efficiency by delivering food to tables

Expenditure: The amount spent

Fine Dining: A restaurant experience with a formal atmosphere and high-quality food that caters to upscale customers

Flambé: Food covered with liquor and set on fire

Food Poisoning: Sickness caused by consuming spoiled food

Garnish: Decoration on a plate or drink

Head Waiter: The person in charge of a restaurant's waitstaff

Hors d'oeuvres: A small dish or portion of food

Host/Hostess: The person in charge of welcoming and seating guests in a restaurant

IRS: The Internal Revenue Service

Liability: Being under obligation or debt

Maître d': The person in charge of the dining room service

Menu: List of dishes served at a restaurant

Portion: A specific amount of something

Strain: An injury generally caused by overexertion or misuse of a muscle

Voucher: A piece of paper that entitles the holder to a discount

Wages: The amount of money received or paid for work

Wine Steward: The waiter who serves and helps patrons choose wine

Appendix

Bibliography

"Casual Dining vs. Fine Dining." *WebstaurantStore*. WebstaurantStore, 30 Sept. 2016. Web. 07 Dec. 2016.

"Food Prices and Spending." US Department of Agriculture, 2016. Web. 07 Dec. 2016.

"Infographics." *National Restaurant Association*. 2016. Web. 07 Dec. 2016.

"Restaurant Facts: 12 Things You Didn't Know." *Reserve*. 07 Oct. 2016. Web. 07 Dec. 2016.

"Restaurant Industry in the U.S." *Statista*. 2016. Web. 06 Dec. 2016.

"Statistics and Facts on Eating out Behavior in the U.S." *Statista*. 2016. Web. 06 Dec. 2016.

Chocano, Carina. "The Chef at 15." The New York Times Magazine. The New York Times, 28 Mar. 2014. Web. 3 Jan. 2017.

Furino, Giaco. "Neuroscience Explains 'Waitmares'" *Mental_floss*. Mental_floss, 9 July 2015. Web. 06 Dec. 2016.

Janofsky, Michael. "Domino's Ends Fast-Pizza Pledge After Big Award to Crash Victim." The New York Times. The New York Times, 22 Dec. 1993. Web. 03 Jan. 2017.

Lord, Bronte. "Record-setting Whisky Sells for $628,205 at Hong Kong Auction." *CNNMoney*. Cable News Network, 21 Jan. 2014. Web. 13 Dec. 2016.

Lynn, M. (1996). Seven ways to increase servers' tips [Electronic version]. Cornell Hotel and Restaurant Administration Quarterly, 37(3), 24-29. Retrieved 6 December 2016, from Cornell University, School of Hospitality Administration site: **http://scholarship.sha.cornell.edu/articles/111**

Malin, Joshua. "The 20 Most Popular Imported Beers In America." *VinePair*. VinePair Inc., 29 Oct. 2015. Web. 16 Dec. 2016.

McGough, Will. "Where Did the Term "86" Come From?" *Mental Floss*. Mental Floss, 13 Aug. 2013. Web. 06 Dec. 2016.

Mealey, Lorri. "10 Things You Don't Know About Restaurants." *The Balance*. 14 Aug. 2016. Web. 06 Dec. 2016.

Porges, Seth. "6 Things You (Probably) Didn't Know About Cognac." *Forbes*. Forbes Magazine, 10 Oct. 2013. Web. 13 Dec. 2016.

Shin, Laura. "The Ultimate Guide To Living On Tips, Part 1: How To Earn More In Tips." *Forbes*. Forbes Magazine, 30 Apr. 2014. Web. 06 Dec. 2016.

The Waitress Confessions. "The Pros and Cons of Being a Waiter / Waitress." The Waitress Confessions. 29 Apr. 2015. Web. 06 Dec. 2016.

Teeter, Adam. "The Difference Between Porter And Stout Beer: It's Complicated." *VinePair*. VinePair Inc., 30 Jan. 2015. Web. 13 Dec. 2016.

"Whisky or Whiskey?" *What Is the Difference between Whisky and Whiskey?* Whisky for Everyone, 2011. Web. 13 Dec. 2016.

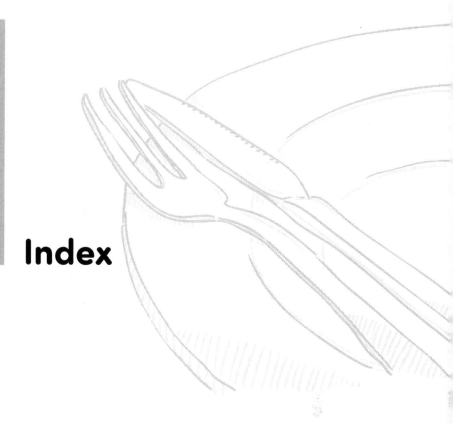

Index